Vintage Knit Gloves and Mittens

25 Patterns for Timeless Fashions

Kathryn Fulton

Photographs by Alan Wycheck and Tiffany Blackstone

STACKPOLE BOOKS

0 11557 01243 9

Published by
STACKPOLE BOOKS
5067 Ritter Road
Mechanicsburg, PA 17055
www.stackpolebooks.com

Printed in the United States of America

10 9 8 7 6 5 4 3 2 1

First edition

Cover design by Tessa J. Sweigert
Photos by Alan Wychek except as indicated.
Photos by Tiffany Blackstone: pages 7, 26, 28 (bottom),
31, 34, 41, 51, 53 (bottom), 55, 93 (bottom).

Library of Congress Cataloging-in-Publication Data

Fulton, Kathryn, 1987–
  Vintage knit gloves and mittens : 25 patterns for
timeless fashions / Kathryn Fulton ; Photographs by Alan
Wycheck and Tiffany Blackstone. —
First edition.
     pages cm
  Includes index.
  ISBN 978-0-8117-1243-9
1. Knitting—Patterns. 2. Gloves. 3. Mittens. I. Title.
TT825.F845 2013
  746.43'2—dc23
                         2013023541

Contents

Classic Mittens

SKILL LEVEL

2-needle

EASY

4-needle

INTERMEDIATE

For decades, knitters have been using this classic, versatile pattern to make mittens for their families and friends. This pattern comes in two options: one worked flat with two straight needles and one worked in the round on double-pointeds. Because of all the sizing options, the pattern is given as an easy-to-follow chart—simply read the text in the left-hand column until you get to a "..." then go to the column for the size you are working to find the number to fill in the blank.

YARN

Pattons Classic Wool (100% pure new wool; 210 yd/192 m; 100 g/3.5 oz) in bright red (1 skein)

NEEDLES

1 set size 4/3.5 mm double-pointed or straight needles *or size needed to obtain gauge*

NOTIONS

Scrap yarn
Yarn needle (for 2-needle version)

MEASUREMENTS

Child small: 7" long
Child medium: 8" long
Child large: 9" long
Adult medium: 10" long
Adult large: 11 1/2" long

GAUGE

6 sts / 8 rounds or rows = 1"

PATTERNS

Two-Needle Mittens	Child small	Child medium	Child large	Adult medium	Adult large
RIGHT MITTEN					
Cuff					
Cast on … sts.	32	36	40	44	48
Work k2, p2 ribbing for … inches,	2½	2½	3	3	3½
decreasing … sts in last row.	1	2	2	2	0
There will be … sts on needles.	31	34	38	42	48
Thumb Gusset					
Beginning with k row, work stockinette st for … rows.	4	4	4	0	0
Inc row 1 for thumb gusset: K … sts,	15	17	19	21	24
inc 1 st in next st (first thumb st), k1, inc 1 st in next st (last thumb st), k rem … sts.	13	15	16	18	21
Work even … rows.	1	1	1	3	3
Inc row 2: K … sts,	15	17	19	21	24
inc 1 st in next st, k3, inc 1 st in next st, k to end. (… sts total.)	35	38	42	46	52
Continue in this pattern, increasing in the first and last thumb st every … rows,	2	2	2	4	4
having 2 more sts in between increases after each inc row, increasing … more times	2	2	3	4	5
for … total sts.	39	42	48	54	62
Dividing row: Knit … sts	15	17	19	21	24
and place on a stitch holder or piece of scrap yarn (back of hand).					
Knit the … thumb sts.	11	11	13	15	17
Place the rem … sts on a holder (palm).	13	14	16	18	21
Thumb					
Turn, purl the thumb sts, cast on loosely pwise … sts.	2	2	2	3	3
Continue to work these … sts in stockinette st	13	13	15	18	20

Two-Needle Mittens *continued*	Child small	Child medium	Child large	Adult medium	Adult large
until thumb measures … inches above cast-on sts.	1¼	1½	1¾	2	2¼
End with a purl row, decreasing … sts on last row.	1	1	0	0	2
Dec row 1: *K1, k2tog. Repeat from * to end.					
Purl 1 row.					
Dec row 2: K2tog across row.					
Break yarn, draw through rem sts, and fasten off. Sew thumb seam.					

Hand

	Child small	Child medium	Child large	Adult medium	Adult large
Take up sts for back of hand, join yarn in last st, pick up and k … sts on cast-on sts for thumb.	2	2	2	3	3
Take up and knit sts for palm. (… sts)	30	33	37	42	48
Work even in stockinette st until piece measures … inches above ribbing	4	5	5½	6	7
or until piece is … inch less than desired length.	½	½	½	1	1
End with a purl row, decreasing … sts in last row.	2	1	1	2	0
Dec row 1: *K2, k2tog. Repeat from * to end of round.					
Knit even … rows.	1	1	1	3	3
Dec row 2: *K1, k2tog. Repeat from * to end of round.					
Knit even … rows.	1	1	1	3	3
Dec round 3: K2tog all the way around.					
Break yarn, draw through rem sts, and fasten off. Sew side seam and weave in all ends.					

LEFT MITTEN

	Child small	Child medium	Child large	Adult medium	Adult large
Work same as right mitten until inc row 1.					
Inc row 1 for thumb gusset: K … sts,	13	14	16	18	21
inc 1 st in next st (first thumb st), k1, inc 1 st in next st (last thumb st), k rem … sts.	15	17	19	21	24
Continue increasing in this pattern as for right mitten until dividing row.					
Dividing row: Knit … sts	13	14	16	18	21
and place on a stitch holder or piece of scrap yarn (palm).					
Knit the … thumb sts.	11	11	13	15	17
Place the rem … sts on a holder (back of hand).	15	17	19	21	24
Finish as for right mitten.					

Four-Needle Mittens	Child small	Child medium	Child large	Adult medium	Adult large
Cuff					
Cast on and divide on 3 needles …sts	32	36	40	44	48
Join to work in round, being careful not to twist sts.					
Work k2, p2 ribbing for …inches,	2½	2½	3	3	3½
decreasing …sts in the last round	1	2	2	2	0
(…sts)	31	34	38	42	48
Hand					
Knit even in stockinette st for …rounds	3	3	3	4	4
First inc. round for thumb: Inc 1 st in first st (first thumb st), k1, inc 1 st in next st (last thumb st), k to end of round. (…sts)	33	36	40	44	50
Knit 2 rounds even.					
Second inc. round: Inc 1 st in first st, k3, inc 1 st in next st, k to end of round. (…sts)	35	38	42	46	52
Continue to inc 1 st in first and last thumb st every third round …times,	2	2	3	4	4
Having 2 more sts between incs after each inc round. (…sts)	39	42	48	54	62
Knit 2 rounds even. Slip to a strand of yarn the …thumb sts.	11	11	13	15	17

Four-Needle Mittens *continued*	Child small	Child medium	Child large	Adult medium	Adult large
At end of last round, cast on … sts.	2	2	3	4	5
There will be … sts on needles.	30	33	37	42	48
Work even until piece measures … inches above ribbing	4	4¾	5¼	6	6¾
or until … inch(es) less than desired length.	½	¾	¾	1	1¼
Decrease … sts in last round.	2	1	1	2	0
Dec round 1: *K2, k2tog. Repeat from * to end of round.					
Knit even … rounds.	1	2	2	3	4
Dec round 2: *K1, k2tog. Repeat from * to end of round.					
Knit even … rounds.	0	1	1	3	4
Dec round 3: K2tog all the way around.					
Break yarn, draw through rem sts, and fasten off.					

Thumb

	Child small	Child medium	Child large	Adult medium	Adult large
Slip to two needles the … thumb sts.	11	11	13	15	17
With a third needle, pick up and knit the … cast-on sts.	2	2	2	3	3
There will be … sts total on the needles for the thumb.	13	13	15	18	20
Knit around until thumb measures … inches above cast-on sts,	1¼	1½	1¾	2	2½
decreasing … sts in last round.	1	1	0	0	0
Dec round 1: *K1, k2tog. Repeat from * to end of round.					
Knit even … rounds.	1	1	1	2	2
Dec round 2: K2tog all the way around.					
Break yarn, draw through rem sts, and fasten off. Weave in all ends.					
Make other mitten in the same way.					

Variation: Safety Mittens

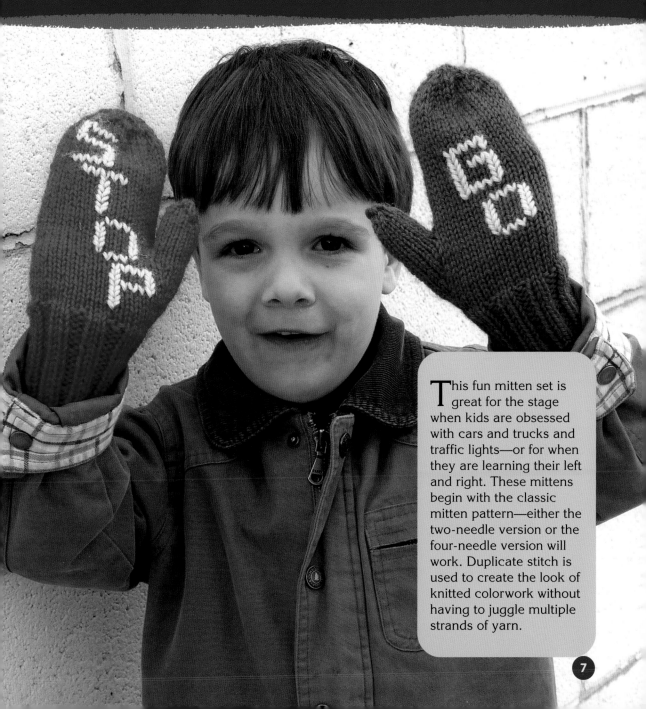

This fun mitten set is great for the stage when kids are obsessed with cars and trucks and traffic lights—or for when they are learning their left and right. These mittens begin with the classic mitten pattern—either the two-needle version or the four-needle version will work. Duplicate stitch is used to create the look of knitted colorwork without having to juggle multiple strands of yarn.

4
Medium

YARN
Knit Picks Wool of the Andes
(100% Peruvian Highland Wool;
110 yds; 50 g) in grass (1 skein),
red (1 skein), and oyster
heather (1 skein)

NOTIONS
Scrap yarn
Yarn needle

PATTERN

Make a pair of classic mittens in the size and
   pattern of your choice (either 2-needle or 4-
   needle). Make the left mitten in red and the
   right mitten in green.

Use duplicate stitch to embroider the word STOP
   on the left mitten and GO on the right mitten in
   white, following the chart on page 10.

Classic Gloves

These gloves feature a subtle pattern of purl stitches on the hand section, but for a classic look you could work the entire hand in stockinette stitch. They are simple enough to be great for men in darks and neutrals, but make them in bright colors or stripes and kids will love them.

2
Fine

YARN
100% wool sport-weight yarn, gray

NEEDLES
1 set size 1/2.25 mm double-pointed needles
or size needed to obtain gauge

NOTIONS
Scrap yarn

MEASUREMENTS
Child small: 7" long
Child medium: 7$\frac{1}{2}$" long
Child large: 8$\frac{3}{4}$" long
Adult medium: 10" long
Adult large: 10$\frac{3}{4}$" long

GAUGE
8 sts / 13 rounds = 1"

PATTERN

	Child small	Child medium	Child large	Adult medium	Adult large

RIGHT GLOVE

Cuff

	Child small	Child medium	Child large	Adult medium	Adult large
Cast on and divide on 3 needles … sts.	36	40	44	52	60
Join, work around in k 2, p 2 ribbing for … inches,	2	2	2½	3	3
increasing … sts in last round.	2	2	3	0	0
(… sts)	38	42	47	52	60

Hand

Round 1: K.

Round 2: Inc 1 st in first st (first thumb st), k 1, inc
1 st in next st (last thumb st), k to end of round.

Round 3: K 5 thumb sts; k 1, *p 1, k 1; repeat from
* to end of round.

Round 4: K.

Round 5: Inc 1 st in first st, k 3, inc 1 st in next st, k to
end of round.

Round 6: K 7 thumb sts; p 1, *k 1, p 1; repeat from
* to end of round.

Round 7: K.

Round 8: Inc 1 st in first st, k 5, inc 1 st in next st,
k to end of round.

Round 9: K 9 thumb sts, k 1, *p 1, k 1; repeat from
* to end of round.

Round 10: K.

Round 11: Inc 1 st in first st, k 7, inc 1 st in next st,
k to end of round.

	Child small	Child medium	Child large	Adult medium	Adult large
Continue to work thumb sts in stockinette st and remaining sts in pattern as in last 6 rounds, increasing 1 st each side of thumb gusset every 3rd round … times,	2	3	4	5	6
having 2 sts more between incs after each successive inc round. (… sts,	50	56	63	70	80

continued	Child small	Child medium	Child large	Adult medium	Adult large
…sts in thumb gusset)	15	17	19	21	23
For men's size only: Work 2 rounds even after last inc round.					
Next round for all sizes: Work first st, slip next …sts	13	15	17	19	21
to a strand of yarn for thumb; cast on for inner side of thumb …sts.	3	3	4	5	5
Work even in pattern on all sts until …inches above sts cast on for inner side of thumb. Discontinue pattern.	1½	1½	1¾	2	2¼
First Finger					
K first …sts,	6	6	7	8	8
slip next …sts	29	32	37	41	47
to a strand of yarn for the other 3 fingers; cast on 3 sts for gusset of first finger, k remaining …sts.	5	6	6	7	9
Join and divide on 3 needles. (…sts)	14	15	16	18	20
K around in stockinette st for …inches or until ¼ inch less than desired length.	1¾	2	2¼	2½	2¾
† **For adult sizes only:** *K2tog, k …sts, repeat from * around. K even for 1 round.	—	—	—	7	3
Next round for all sizes: *K2tog, k …sts, repeat from * to end of round. (12 sts)	5	3	2	2	2
K 1 round even.					
Last round: K2tog 6 times; break off, leaving an end; draw end through remaining 6 sts twice. Fasten off.					
Second Finger					
Slip from back of hand to needle …sts.	5	5	6	7	9
Join yarn; pick up and k 3 sts on gusset of first finger; take up and k …sts	4	5	6	7	8
from palm of hand. Cast on 3 sts for gusset; join and divide on 3 needles. (…sts)	15	16	18	20	23
K around for …inches or until ¼ inch less than desired length.	2	2¼	2½	2¾	3
Next round: K, decreasing …sts evenly in the round,	1	1	2	2	3
leaving …sts.	14	15	16	18	20
Finish as for first finger, from † onward.					

continued

	Child small	Child medium	Child large	Adult medium	Adult large
Third Finger					
Slip from back of hand to needle . . . sts.	5	5	6	7	7
Join yarn; pick up and k 3 sts on gusset of second finger; take up and k . . . sts	4	5	5	6	7
from palm of hand. Cast on . . . sts for gusset;	2	2	2	2	3
join and divide on 3 needles. (. . . sts)	14	15	16	18	20
K around for . . . inches	1¾	2	2¼	2½	2¾

or until ¼ inch less than desired length.
Finish as for first finger, from † onward.

continued	Child small	Child medium	Child large	Adult medium	Adult large
Fourth Finger					
Slip remaining … sts	11	12	14	14	16
to 2 needles. Join yarn; pick up and k … sts	2	2	2	2	3
on gusset of third finger on third needle; join.					
(… sts)	13	14	16	16	19
K around for … inches	1¼	1½	1¾	2	2¼
or until ¼ inch less than desired length.					
For men's size only: K 1 round, decreasing 3 sts					
evenly.					
K 1 round even (12 sts).					
Next round for all sizes: Finish as for first finger,					
from † onward.					
Thumb					
Slip … thumb sts	13	15	17	19	21
from their piece of yarn to 2 needles. Pick up					
and k … sts	5	5	6	7	7
on sts cast on for inner side of thumb. (… sts)	18	20	23	26	28
*K 1 round even.					
Next round: K, decreasing 1 st at center of picked					
up sts.					
Repeat from * … times.	2	3	4	5	5
(… sts)	15	16	18	20	22
Work remaining sts even until … inches	1½	1¾	2	2¼	2½
above picked up sts, or about ¼ inch less than					
desired length.					
Next round: K, decreasing … sts	1	1	2	2	3
evenly over round. (… sts)	14	15	16	18	20
Finish as for first finger, from † onward.					
Weave in all ends.					
LEFT GLOVE					
Work same as right glove up to hand. (… sts)	38	42	47	52	60

Hand

Round 1: K.

Round 2: K to 3 sts from end of round, inc 1 st in
   next st (first thumb st), k 1, inc 1 st in next st (last thumb st).

continued

	Child small	Child medium	Child large	Adult medium	Adult large
Round 3: K 1, *p 1, k 1; repeat from * to 5 sts from end, k 5.					
Round 4: K.					
Round 5: K to 5 sts from end of round, inc 1 st in next st, k 3, inc 1 st in last st.					
Round 6: P 1, *k 1, p 1; repeat from * to 7 sts from end, k 7.					
Continue to work thumb sts in stockinette st and remaining sts in pattern, increasing 1 st each side of thumb gusset every 3rd round … more times,	4	5	6	7	8
having 2 sts more between incs after each successive inc round. (… sts,	50	56	63	70	80
… sts in thumb gusset)	15	17	19	21	23
For men's size only: Work 2 rounds even after last inc round.					
Next round for all sizes: Work to … sts	14	16	18	20	22
from end of round, slip next … sts	13	15	17	19	21
to a strand of yarn for thumb. Cast on … sts	3	3	4	5	5
for inner side of thumb, work last st of round. (… sts)	40	44	50	56	64
Work even in pattern on all sts until same length as right glove. Discontinue pattern.					

First Finger

	Child small	Child medium	Child large	Adult medium	Adult large
K first … sts	5	6	6	7	9
slip next … sts	29	32	37	41	47
to a strand of yarn for the other 3 fingers; cast on 3 sts for gusset of first finger, k remaining … sts.	6	6	7	8	9
Join and divide on 3 needles. (… sts)	14	15	16	18	20

Finish as for first finger of right glove.

Other Fingers

Work as on right glove.

Mock Cable Mittens

SKILL LEVEL

INTERMEDIATE

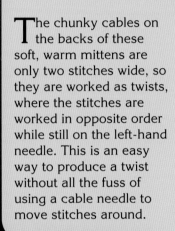

The chunky cables on the backs of these soft, warm mittens are only two stitches wide, so they are worked as twists, where the stitches are worked in opposite order while still on the left-hand needle. This is an easy way to produce a twist without all the fuss of using a cable needle to move stitches around.

5
Bulky

YARN
Plymouth Encore Chunky
(75% acrylic, 25% wool; 143 yd;
3.5 oz/100 g) in #2426 (purple)

NEEDLES
1 set size 10/6 mm straight needles *or size
needed to obtain gauge*

NOTIONS
Stitch holders or pieces of scrap yarn (2)
Yarn needle

MEASUREMENTS
10" long

GAUGE
7 sts = 2"; 5 rows = 1"

SPECIAL STITCH
Left twist (LT): Knit the second stitch on the
left-hand needle through the back of the
loop and leave it on the needle. Knit the
first stitch as normal, then slide both sts
off the needle.

PATTERN

RIGHT MITTEN

Cuff

Cast on 26 sts.

Row 1: P14, [k2, p2] 3 times.

Row 2: K2, p2, LT, p2, LT, p2, k14.

Rows 3–15: Repeat rows 1 and 2, ending with a
    row 1.

Thumb Gusset

Row 16: K2, p2, LT, p2, LT, p2, k2, kfb, k1, kfb, k9.

Row 17: P16, [k2, p2] 3 times.

Row 18: K2, p2, LT, p2, LT, p2, k2, kfb, k3, kfb, k9.

Row 19: P18, [k2, p2] 3 times.

Row 20: K2, p2, LT, p2, LT, p2, k2, kfb, k5, kfb, k9.

Row 21: P20, [k2, p2] 3 times.

Row 22: K2, p2, LT, p2, LT, p2, k2, kfb, k7, kfb, k9.

Row 23: P22, [k2, p2] 3 times.

Row 24: K2, p2, LT, p2, LT, p2, k3; place these sts on a
    stitch holder or piece of scrap yarn. Knit next 9
    sts; place rem 10 sts on a stitch holder.

Thumb

Cast on 1 st at the end of the 9 sts.

Row 1: Turn and purl back, cast on 1 st pwise at the
    other end. (11 sts)

Row 2: Knit.

Row 3: Purl.

Rows 4–11: Repeat rows 2 and 3.

Row 12: K2tog across.

Break yarn, pull end through rem sts, and fasten off.
    Sew side seam of thumb.

Hand

Take up the sts from the first stitch holder. Join yarn
    and pick up and knit 4 sts along bottom of
    thumb; then take up and knit the sts from the
    second stitch holder.

Row 25: P15, [k2, p2] 3 times.

Row 26: K2, p2, LT, p2, LT, p2, k15.

Rows 27–43: Repeat rows 25 and 26, ending with a
    row 25.

Row 44: K2, p2tog, LT, p2tog, LT, p2tog, *k2, k2tog;
    repeat from * to end.

Row 45: P10, [k1, p2] 3 times.
Row 46: K2tog across.
Break yarn, pull through rem sts, and fasten off. Sew
    side seam and weave in ends.

LEFT MITTEN
Cuff
Cast on 26 sts.
Row 1: [P2, k2] 3 times, p14.
Row 2: K14, p2, LT, p2, LT, p2, k2.
Rows 3–15: Repeat rows 1 and 2, ending with a
    row 1.

Thumb Gusset
Row 16: K9, kfb, k1, kfb, k2, p2, LT, p2, LT, p2, k2.
Row 17: [P2, k2] 3 times, p16.
Row 18: K9, kfb, k3, kfb, k2, p2, LT, p2, LT, p2, k2.
Row 19: [P2, k2] 3 times, p18.
Row 20: K9, kfb, k5, kfb, k2, p2, LT, p2, LT, p2, k2.
Row 21: [P2, k2] 3 times, p20.
Row 22: K9, kfb, k7, kfb, k2, p2, LT, p2, LT, p2, k2.
Row 23: [P2, k2] 3 times, p22.
Row 24: K10, place on a stitch holder; k9, place rem
    sts on a stitch holder.

Thumb
Work as for right mitten.

Hand
Take up the sts from the first stitch holder. Join yarn
    and pick up and knit 4 sts along bottom of
    thumb; then take up and work the sts from the
    second stitch holder as follows: k3, p2, LT, p2, LT,
    p2, k2.
Row 25: [P2, k2] 3 times, p15.
Row 26: K15, p2, LT, p2, LT, p2, k2.
Rows 27–43: Repeat rows 25 and 26, ending with a
    row 25.
Row 44: [K2tog, k2] 5 times, p2tog, LT, p2tog, LT,
    p2tog, k2.

Row 45: [P2, k1] 3 times, p10.
Row 46: K2tog across.
Break yarn, pull through rem sts, and fasten off. Sew
    side seam.

Mittens

*F*rostrosen, the snowflakelike flowers on the fronts and backs of these mittens, are a classic motif in Nordic knitting. In a lightweight yarn, as shown here, these mittens will fit an average woman's hands; for a larger size, try a worsted-weight yarn. (For a similar mitten in even lighter-weight yarn, see the Oslo mittens on page 59.)

3
Light

YARN
Plymouth Encore DK (75% acrylic, 25% wool; 150 yd; 1.75 oz/50 g)
A: navy (1 skein)
B: white (1 skein)

NEEDLES
1 set size 3/3.25 mm double-pointed needles
   or size needed to obtain gauge

NOTIONS
Stitch holder or scrap yarn

MEASUREMENTS
11" long

GAUGE
7 sts / 8 rounds = 1"

PATTERN

Cuff

With A, cast on 48 sts. Join to work in round.

Work in k2, p2 ribbing for 5 rows of A, then 4 rows of B, 2 rows of A, 2 rows of B, 2 rows of A, 2 rows of B, 2 rows of A, 4 rows of B, and 4 rows of A, increasing 1 st in last row.

Hand

Begin Fair Isle pattern. Work in stockinette st, following chart for the colors. Always carry the yarn not in use on the wrong side of the work.

Follow chart until round 18.

> **Round 18 is the only round in this pattern that is different on the left and right mittens. The rest of the mittens are identical.**

Round 18 (left mitten): Work first 26 sts of chart; break B; place next 10 sts on a stitch holder or piece of scrap yarn for the thumb. Cast on 10 sts with A; join B; work last 12 sts of chart.

Round 18 (right mitten): Work first 13 sts of chart; break B; place next 10 sts on a stitch holder or piece of scrap yarn for the thumb. Cast on 10 sts with A; join B; work last 25 sts of chart.

Continue to follow chart until round 48.

Round 48: With A, k1, k3tog, work next 18 sts of chart, k2tog, k1, k3tog; work next 17 sts of chart, k2tog, k1.

Round 49: K1, k2tog, work next 16 sts of chart, k2tog, k1, k2tog, work next 15 sts of chart, k2tog, k1.

Round 50: K1, k2tog, work next 14 sts of chart, k2tog, k1, k2tog, work next 13 sts of chart, k2tog, k1.

Round 51: K1, k2tog, work next 12 sts of chart, k2tog, k1, k2tog, work next 11 sts of chart, k2tog, k1.

Round 52: With A, k1, k2tog, k10, k2tog, k1, k9, k2tog, k1.

Sew remaining sts together with the kitchener stitch.

Thumb

Slip the 10 thumb sts from holder to needle; join A,
  cast on 10 sts. Divide these 20 sts on 3 needles
  and join to work in round.
Round 1: *K1 in A, k1 in B; repeat from * around.
Round 2: *K1 in B, k1 in A; repeat from * around.
Repeat these 2 rounds until the thumb measures
  2½ inches from the cast-on sts. Break B.
Dec round 1: With A, k2tog around.
Knit 1 round even.
Last round: K2tog around.
Break yarn, draw end through rem sts, and fasten
  off. Weave in ends.

= Color A

= Color B

The playful clowns on these mittens for a younger child are a great way to use up leftover scraps of bright-colored yarn. The mittens are worked flat on two needles because of the intarsia sections.

Fine 2

YARN
Cascade Yarns Cascade 220 Sport (100% Peruvian highland wool; 164 yd/150 m; 50 g/ 1.75 oz) in

A: navy (1 skein)
B: palm (1 skein)
C: magenta (1 skein)
D: yellow (1 skein)
E: white (1 skein)

NEEDLES
1 set size 2/2.75 mm straight needles *or size needed to obtain gauge*

NOTIONS
12 bobbins
Scrap yarn or stitch holder

MEASUREMENTS
Small: 7½" long
Medium: 8¼" long
Large: 9½" long

GAUGE
7 sts / 10 rnds = 1"

Wind the yarn onto multiple small bobbins:
3 each for colors A and E and 2 each for
colors B, C, and D. Save a ball of A
in addition to the 3 bobbins.

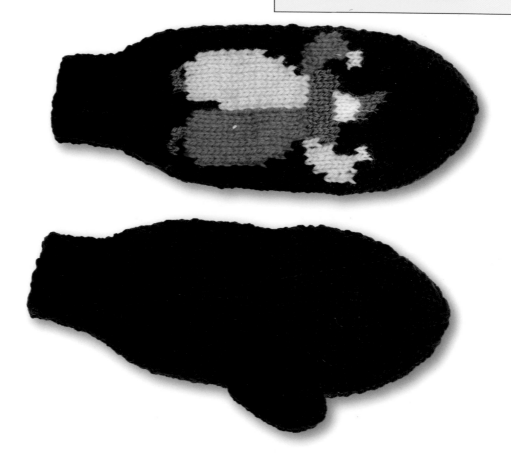

PATTERN

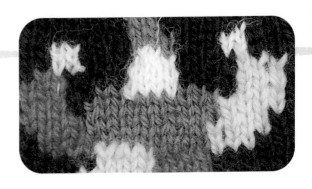

Instructions are for a small (2–4 years), with instructions for medium (5–7) and large (8–10) in brackets.

RIGHT MITTEN

Cuff

With ball of A, cast on 36 {40, 44} sts loosely. Work
  k2, p2 ribbing for 2½ {2½, 3} inches.

Knit one row, increasing 4 sts evenly spread across
  row. (40 {44, 48} sts)

Work even in stockinette st for 1 {3, 5} rows. Break
  off yarn; join first bobbin of A.

Hand

Row 1: With A, k4 {5, 6}; with bobbin of B, k 4; with
  2nd bobbin of A, k4; with 2nd bobbin of B, k4;
  with ball of A k24 {27, 30}.

Row 2: With ball of A, p24; k4 with B; k4 with A; k4
  with B; k4 {5, 6} with A.

> **To prevent a hole when changing colors, bring the new color under the last color used.**

Continue to work in stockinette st, following chart on page 30 for colors and using a separate bobbin for each section of color, until 18 {20, 22} rows above ribbing.

Dividing row: Work 21 {23, 25} sts, place on holder or piece of scrap yarn for back of hand, k next 7 {8, 9} sts for thumb, place rem sts on holder for palm.

Thumb

Turn; with A, purl the 7 {8, 9} thumb sts, cast on 7 {8, 9} sts loosely for other side of thumb. (14 {16, 18} sts).

Work even until 1 1/4 {1 1/2, 1 3/4} inches above cast-on sts, ending with a purl row.

Next row: Knit, decreasing 2 {4, 6} sts evenly across row. (12 sts)

New row: Purl.

Next row: K2tog across row. (6 sts)

Break yarn, draw end through rem sts, fasten off.

Sew thumb seam.

Hand Finishing

Take up sts for back of hand; join A in last st. With same needle, pick up and k 7 {8, 9} sts along bottom cast-on edge of thumb. Take up and knit palm sts to same needle. (40 {44, 48} sts)

Continue in stockinette stitch, following color chart.

At end of chart, break off all bobbins. Continue with ball of A, working even in stockinette st until piece measures 4 1/4 {4 3/4, 5 1/4} inches above ribbing. End with a purl row.

Next row: Knit, decreasing 4 {2, 0} sts evenly across row. (36 {42, 48} sts)

Dec row 1: *K4 {5, 6}, k2tog; repeat from * to end of row. (30 {36, 42} sts)

Next row: Purl.

Dec row 2: *K3 {4, 5}, k2tog; repeat from * to end of row. (24 {30, 36} sts)

Next row: Purl.

Continue in this pattern, decreasing every other row, with 1 fewer st between decreases on each dec row, until 18 sts remain. (3 {4, 5} total dec rows)

Purl 1 row after last dec row.

Last row: K2tog across row.

Break yarn, draw end through rem sts, and fasten off.

Sew side seam and weave in ends.

LEFT MITTEN

Work same as for right mitten up to beg of hand. Do not break off ball of A.

Hand

Row 1: With ball of A, k24 {27, 30}; with bobbin of B, k4; with bobbin of A, k4; with 2nd bobbin of B, k4; with 2nd bobbin of A, k4 {5, 6}.

Row 2: P4 {5, 6} with A; p4 with B; p4 with A; p4 with B; p24 {27, 30} with A.

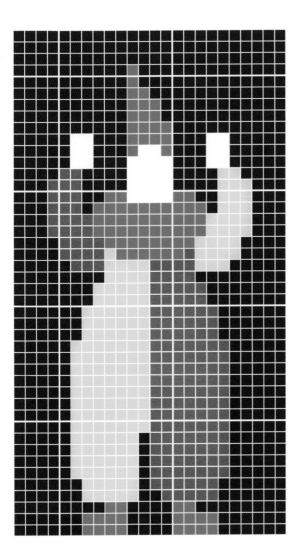

Continue to work in stockinette st, following chart for colors and using a separate bobbin for each section of color, until 17 {19, 21} rows above ribbing.

Dividing row: Work 21 {23, 25} sts, place on holder or piece of scrap yarn for back of hand, k next 7 {8, 9} sts for thumb, place rem sts on holder for palm.

Thumb

Turn; with A, knit the 7 {8, 9} thumb sts, cast on 7 {8, 9} sts loosely for other side of thumb. (14 {16, 18} sts). Finish as for right mitten.

Hand

Take up palm sts; join A at inner edge and purl to end.

Next row: K palm sts. With same needle, pick up and k 7 {8, 9} sts along bottom cast-on edge of thumb. Take up and knit sts for back of hand to same needle. (40 {44, 48} sts)

Finish as for right mitten.

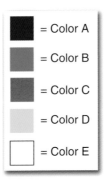

■ = Color A

■ = Color B

■ = Color C

▢ = Color D

□ = Color E

Convertible Mittens

From the days of buttoned shoes and buckled harnesses to today's era of smartphones and car keys, people have always needed mittens that keep hands warm while allowing use of the fingers. A ribbed underflap overlaps with the palm to block drafts getting in through the opening, then folds over when these mittens are "open" to hug the top part against the back of the hand without the need for a button.

YARN
Knit Picks Wool of the Andes
(100% Peruvian Highland Wool;
110 yds; 50 g) in Lava Heather
(1 skein), Cobblestone Heather (1 skein),
and Dove Heather (2 skeins)

NEEDLES
1 set size 4/3.5 mm double-pointed needles
or size needed to obtain gauge

NOTIONS
Stitch holder or scrap yarn

MEASUREMENTS
10½" long

GAUGE
6 sts / 9 rounds = 1"

PATTERN

LEFT MITTEN

Cuff

With A, cast on 40 sts. Divide on three needles and
join to work in round.

Rounds 1–4: *K2, p2; repeat from * around.

Round 5: With B, knit.

Rounds 6–8: With B, *k2, p2; repeat from * around.

Rounds 9–12: Repeat rounds 5–8 with C.

Rounds 13–16: Repeat rounds 5–8 with A.

Rounds 17–20: Repeat rounds 5–8 with B.

Rounds 21–24: Repeat rounds 5–8 with C,
increasing 2 sts in the last round. (42 sts)

Break B and C.

Thumb Gusset

Rounds 25–28: With A, knit.

Round 29: Kfb, k1, kfb, knit to end of round.

Rounds 30–31: Knit.

Round 32: Kfb, k3, kfb, knit to end of round.

Rounds 33–34: Knit.

Round 35: Kfb, k5, kfb, knit to end of round.

Rounds 36–37: Knit.

Round 38: Kfb, k7, kfb, knit to end of round.

Rounds 39–40: Knit.

Round 41: Kfb, k9, kfb, knit to end of round.

Rounds 42–43: Knit.

Round 44: Kfb, k11, kfb, knit to end of round.

Rounds 45–46: Knit.

Hand

Setup for hand: Slip first 15 sts to a stitch holder or
piece of scrap yarn for the thumb. Cast on 3 sts
and place them on the right-hand needle. Place
the first 10 sts after the cast-on sts on one
needle, the next 10 sts on another needle, and
the rem 22 sts on a third needle for the palm.

Rounds 47–56: Knit.

Rounds 57–61: K20, *p2, k2; repeat from * to end of
round.

Round 62 (dividing round): K20, leave on needles
for back of hand; bind off next 22 sts in ribbing.
Fasten off.

Underflap

With B, cast on 22.

Row 1: *K2, p2; repeat from * to end of row.

Row 2: *P2, k2; repeat from * to end of row.

Row 3: Repeat row 1.

Row 4: With C, purl.

Rows 5–7: With C, repeat rows 1–3.

Row 8: With A, knit.

Row 9: Purl.

Row 10: Knit.

Row 11: Purl.

Hand Finishing

Round 63 (joining round): Take up the 20 sts set
aside for the back of the mitten. Join B and knit
across. At the end of the 20 sts, continue onto
the 22 sts of the underflap. (42 sts)

Rounds 64–66: With B, knit. Break B.

Rounds 67–70: With A, knit.

Rounds 71–74: With C, knit. Break C.

Rounds 75–78: With A, knit, decreasing 2 sts evenly
in round 78. (40 sts)

Round 79: *K2, k2tog; repeat from * around.

Rounds 80–82: Knit.

Round 83: *K1, k2tog; repeat from * around.

Rounds 84–86: Knit.
Round 87: K2tog around.
Break yarn, draw end through rem sts, and fasten off.

Thumb

Slip the 15 thumb sts to 2 needles; with A and a free needle, pick up and knit 3 sts on the cast-on sts for the top edge of the thumb hole. (18 sts)
Knit even until thumb measures 2 inches above the picked-up sts.

Dec round 1: *K1, k2tog; repeat from * around.
Next 2 rounds: Knit.
Last round: K2tog around.
Break yarn, draw end through rem sts, and fasten off.
Weave in all ends.

RIGHT MITTEN

Work same as left mitten to hand.

Hand

Setup for hand: Slip first 15 sts to a stitch holder or piece of scrap yarn for the thumb. Cast on 3 sts. Place the 3 cast-on sts and the next 19 sts on the first needle for the palm (22 sts in palm), the next 10 sts on the second needle, and the rem 10 sts on the third needle.
Rounds 47–56: Knit.
Rounds 57–61: [P2, k2] 10 times, p2, k20.
Round 62 (dividing round): Bind off first 22 sts in ribbing, knit to end, leaving these 20 rem sts on the needles for the back of the hand. Break yarn.

Underflap

Work as for left mitten.

Hand Finishing

Round 63 (joining round): With B, knit across 22 sts of underflap. Then continue across the 20 sts set aside for back of hand. (42 sts)
Finish top and work thumb as for left mitten.

Leaf-Raking Gloves

Quick and easy to knit, these sturdy fingerless gloves are great for working outside or driving. The simple stitch pattern adds texture and shows up well in a solid-colored yarn.

3

Light

YARN
Elsebeth Lavold Silky Wool XL
(80% wool, 20% silk; 104 yd/
95 m; 50 g) in charcoal (1 skein)

NEEDLES
1 set size 1/2.25 mm double-pointed needles
or size needed to obtain gauge

NOTIONS
Stitch holder or scrap yarn

MEASUREMENTS
7¼" long

GAUGE
5 sts / 8 rounds = 1"

PATTERN

Cuff

Cast on 40 sts. Join to work in round, being careful
not to twist the sts.
Work in k2, p2 ribbing for 3 inches.

Hand

Round 1: *K9, kfb; repeat from * to end of round.
(44 sts)
Round 2: K to last 3 sts, p1, k1, p1 for thumb gusset.
Round 3: *K1, p1; repeat from * to end of round.
Round 4: Knit to last 3 sts, p1, M1, k1, M1, p1.
Round 5: Knit to first p st of thumb gusset, p1, k3, p1.
Round 6: *K1, p1; repeat from * to first p st of
thumb gusset, p2, k1, p2.
Round 7: Knit to first p st of thumb gusset, p1, M1,
k3, M1, p1.
Round 8: Knit to first p st of thumb gusset, p1, k5, p1.
Round 9: *K1, p1; repeat from * to end of round.
Round 10: Knit to first p st of thumb gusset, p1, M1,
k5, M1, p1.
Round 11: Knit to first p st of thumb gusset, p1, k7,
p1.
Round 12: *K1, p1; repeat from * to first p st of
thumb gusset, p2, k1, p1, k1, p1, k1, p2.
Round 13: Knit to first p st of thumb gusset, p1, M1,
k7, M1, p1.
Round 14: Knit to first p st of thumb gusset, p1, k9,
p1.
Round 15: *K1, p1; repeat from * to end of round.
Round 16: Knit to first p st of thumb gusset, p1, M1,
k9, M1, p1.
Round 17: Knit to first p st of thumb gusset, p1, k11,
p1.
Round 18: *K1, p1; repeat from * to first p st of
thumb gusset, p2, k1, p1, k1, p1, k1, p1, k1, p2.
Round 19: Knit to first p st of thumb gusset, p1, M1,
k11, M1, p1.
Round 20: Knit to first p st of thumb gusset, p1, k13,
p1.

Round 21: *K1, p1; repeat from * to end of round.
Round 22: Knit to first p st of thumb gusset; p1, slip
next 13 sts to a piece of scrap yarn for the
thumb; cast on 3 sts, p last st. (46 sts)
Round 23: Knit.
Round 24: *K1, p1; repeat from * to end of round.
Round 25: Knit.
Repeat rounds 23–25 until the hand measures 1½
inches above cast-on sts for top edge of thumb
opening, ending with a round 24.
Ribbing: Work in k2, p2 ribbing for 4 rounds.
Bind off in pattern.

Thumb

Slip the 13 sts for the thumb onto needles; pick up
and knit 5 sts on the 3 cast-on sts for top edge
of thumb opening. (18 sts)
Round 1: K2, p2 around.
Round 2: K2tog, (p2, k2) to last 2 sts, k2tog.
Round 3: K1, (p2, k2) to last st, k1.
Rounds 4–6: Repeat round 3.
Bind off in pattern.
Weave in all ends.

Plaid Gloves

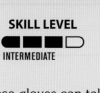
These gloves can take a wide variety of looks, depending on the colors you use for them. In bright, funky colors as shown here, they have a retro flavor; in traditional reds and browns they'll look more like a classic plaid. With the way it highlights the colors, this pattern is great for showcasing a particular color scheme—such as a graduate's school colors.

1

Super Fine

YARN
Cascade Yarns Cascade 220 Fingering (100% Peruvian highland wool; 273 yd/250 m; 50 g/1.75 oz) in
A: Van Dyke brown (1 skein)
B: Jack o'lantern (1 skein)
C: natural (1 skein)
D: highland green (1 skein)

NEEDLES
1 set size 1/2.25 mm double-pointed needles
or size needed to obtain gauge

NOTIONS
Scrap yarn

MEASUREMENTS
9" long

GAUGE
9 sts / 13 rounds = 1"

PATTERN

RIGHT GLOVE

Cuff

With A, cast on 60 sts. Divide onto 3 needles. Work k2, p2 ribbing for 1½ inches. Knit 1 round, increasing 1 st. (61 sts). Break off A; join B.

Hand

Cut 3 strands of C and 3 strands of D, each 30 inches long. Use a separate strand for each change of color.

Round 1: K5 with B, †*k1 C, k10 B, k1 D, k10 B; repeat from * once; end with k1 C, k10 B, k1 D.†

Round 2: Repeat round 1.

> **Continue vertical stripes with same colors up to fingers, working horizontal stripes and shaping thumb gusset as follows.**

Round 3 (first inc round for thumb gusset, right glove): With B, k1, inc 1 st in next st, k1, inc 1 st in next st (5 sts in thumb gusset), k1; repeat between †s of round 1.

Rounds 4–5: With B, k7; repeat between †s of round 1.

Round 6 (second inc round): With B, k1, inc 1 st in next st, k3, inc 1 st in next st (7 sts in thumb gusset), k1; repeat between †s of round 1.

Round 7: With B, k9; repeat between †s of round 1.

Round 8: With separate strand of C, k20 C, k1 D, *k21 C, k1 D; repeat from * once. Break off separate strand of C.

Round 9 (third inc round): With B, k1; inc 1 st in next st, k5, inc 1 st in next st (9 sts in thumb gusset), k1; repeat between †s of round 1.

Round 10: With B, k11; repeat between †s of round 1.

Round 11: With separate strand of C, k22 C, k1 D, *k21 C, k1 D; repeat from * once. Break off separate strand of C.

Round 12 (fourth inc round): With B, k1; inc 1 st in next st, k7, inc 1 st in next st (11 sts in thumb gusset), k1; repeat between †s of round 1.

Continue to increase in this pattern, increasing in the first and last st of thumb gusset every third round, having 2 sts more between increases in each successive inc round, until there are 21 sts in thumb gusset.

Work the next 18 rounds in the following colors, continuing the vertical stripes of C and D and working horizontal stripes of D in round 26 and 29 with separate strands of D (as in round 11).

Round 13: B

Round 14: B

Round 15: B. Increase round (13 sts in thumb gusset).

Round 16: B

Round 17: B

Round 18: B. Increase round (15 sts in thumb gusset).

Round 19: A.

Round 20: A.

Round 21: A. Increase round (17 sts in thumb gusset).

Round 22: A.

Round 23: A.

Round 24: A. Increase round (19 sts in thumb gusset).

Round 25: A.
Round 26: Stripe of D.
Round 27: A. Increase round (21 sts in thumb gusset).
Round 28: A.
Round 29: Stripe of D.
Round 30: With A, k2; place next 19 sts on strand of scrap yarn, cas on 6 sts on right-hand needle, finish round. (66 sts)
Work even in stockinette st.
Rounds 31–36: A.
Rounds 37–43: B.
Round 44: C.
Rounds 45–46: B.
Round 47: C.
Rounds 48–54: B.
Break off all colors; join A.
Round 55: With A, knit whole round.

All fingers are worked only in A.

First Finger

Knit 9 sts, slip next 48 sts to a strand of scrap yarn for 3 rem fingers, leave 9 rem sts on needle for first finger. Cast on 3 sts for gusset. Divide these 21 sts on 3 needles; join to work in round.
Knit around for 2 1/2 inches, decreasing 1 st in last round. (20 sts)
Dec round 1: *K3, k2tog; repeat from * to end of round. (16 sts)
Knit 1 round even.
Dec round 2: *K2, k2tog; repeat from * around. (12 sts)
Knit one round even.
Last round: K2tog across round.
Break off, draw end twice through rem sts, and fasten off.

Second Finger

Slip 8 sts from back of hand from scrap yarn to needle; pick up and knit the 3 cast-on sts at the base of the first finger; knit 8 sts from palm of hand from scrap yarn to needle; cast on 3 sts for gusset. Divide these 22 sts on 3 needles; join to work in round.
Knit around for 2 3/4 inches, decreasing 2 sts in last round. (20 sts)
Finish as for first finger.

Third Finger

Slip 8 sts from back of hand from scrap yarn to needle; pick up and knit the 3 cast-on sts at the base of the second finger; knit 8 sts from palm of hand from scrap yarn to needle; cast on 2 sts for gusset. Divide these 21 sts on 3 needles; join to work in round.
Finish as for first finger.

Fourth Finger

Slip rem 16 sts from thread to needles; pick up and knit the 2 cast-on sts at the base of the third finger. Divide these 18 sts on 3 needles; join to work in round.

Knit around for 2 inches, decreasing 2 sts in last round. (16 sts)

Beginning with decrease round 2, finish as for first finger.

Thumb

Slip the 19 thumb sts to 2 needles; pick up and knit 8 sts on the 6 cast-on sts along the top of the thumb hole. Divide these 27 sts on 3 needles; join to work in round.

*Knit 1 round. On next round, dec 1 st at center of picked-up sts. Repeat from * 4 times. (22 sts)

Work even until 2 inches above picked-up sts.

Finish as for second finger.

Weave in ends.

LEFT GLOVE

Work same as right glove up to beginning of hand. (61 sts)

Round 1: K5 with B, †*k1 D, k10 B, k1 C, k10 B; repeat from * once; end with k1 D, k10 B, k1 C.†

Round 2: Repeat round 1.

Round 3 (first inc round for thumb gusset, right glove): With B, k1, inc 1 st in next st, k1, inc 1 st in next st (5 sts in thumb gusset), k1; repeat between †s of round 1.

Rounds 4–5: With B, k7; repeat between †s of round 1.

Round 6 (second inc round): With B, k1, inc 1 st in next st, k3, inc 1 st in next st (7 sts in thumb gusset), k1; repeat between †s of round 1.

Round 7: With B, k9; repeat between †s of round 1.

Round 8: With separate strand of C, k9 C, *k1 D, k21 C; repeat from * once. Break off separate strand of C.

Continue as for right glove until first finger.

First Finger

K1, sl this st to last needle, k next 18 sts for first finger. Slip next 48 sts to a piece of scrap yarn for 3 rem fingers. Cast on 3 sts for gusset. Divide these 21 sts on 3 needles; join to work in round.

Finish as for first finger of right glove.

Work other fingers and thumb as on right glove.

Canary Mittens

Just like the women's version on page 18, these little mittens use a twist method of making mini cables without the use of a cable needle. This pattern offers three different sizing options, so you can make matching mittens for a mom and a daughter of any age, or for a big and little sister.

43

Medium

YARN
Stitch Nation Washable Ewe
(100% superwash wool,
183 yd/167 m; 3.5 oz/100 g)
in duckling (1 skein)

NEEDLES
1 set size 4/3.75 mm straight needles *or size
needed to obtain gauge*

NOTIONS
Stitch holders or pieces of scrap yarn (2)

MEASUREMENTS
Small: 6½" long
Medium: 7" long
Large: 8" long

GAUGE
5 sts / 8 rows = 1"

SPECIAL STITCH
Left twist (LT): Knit the second stitch on the
left-hand needle through the back of the
loop and leave it on the needle. Knit the
first stitch as normal, then slide both sts
off the needle.

PATTERN

Pattern is for small size (4 years);
instructions for medium (6 years) and
large (8 years) sizes in parentheses.

RIGHT MITTEN
Cuff
Cast on 32 {36, 40} sts.
Work in k1, p1 ribbing for 2½ inches.

Hand
Row 1: K3 {4, 5}, p2, LT, p2, LT, p2, k19 {22, 25}.
Row 2: P19 {22, 25}, k2, p2, k2, p2, k2, p3 {4, 5}.
Rows 3–4: Repeat rows 1–2.
Row 5: K3 {4, 5}, p2, LT, p2, LT, p2, k3 {4, 5}, kfb in each
   of next 2 sts, k14 {16, 18}.
Row 6: P21 {24, 27}, k2, p2, k2, p2, k2, p3 {4, 5}.
Row 7: K3 {4, 5}, p2, LT, p2, LT, p2, k3 {4, 5}, kfb, k2, kfb,
   k14 {16, 18}.
Row 8: P23 {26, 29}, k2, p2, k2, p2, k2, p3 {4, 5}.
Row 9: K3 {4, 5}, p2, LT, p2, LT, p2, k3 {4, 5}, kfb, k4, kfb,
   k14 {16, 18}.
Row 10: P25 {28, 31}, k2, p2, k2, p2, k2, p3 {4, 5}.
Row 11: K3 {4, 5}, p2, LT, p2, LT, p2, k3 {4, 5}, kfb, k6,
   kfb, k14 {16, 18}.
Row 12: P27 {30, 33}, k2, p2, k2, p2, k2, p3 {4, 5}.
Small and medium size, go to row 13; large size
   increase once more as follows:
Final increase row (large size only): K5, p2, LT, p2,
   LT, p2, k5, kfb, k8, kfb, k18.
Next row: P35, k2, p2, k2, p2, k2, p5. Now go to row
   13.
Row 13: K3 {4, 5}, p2, LT, p2, LT, p2, k3 {4, 5}; slip these
   16 {18, 20} sts to a stitch holder or piece of scrap
   yarn. Knit next 10 {10, 12} sts; slip rem 14 {16, 18}
   sts to a second stitch holder.

Thumb
Cast on 1 st at the end of the thumb sts. Turn and
   purl back, cast on 1 st pwise at the other end.
   (12, {12, 14} sts)
Work in stockinette st on these sts until thumb
   measures 1½ {1½, 1¾} inches.
Next row: K2tog across.
Break yarn, draw end through rem sts, and fasten
   off. Sew side seam of thumb.

Hand Finishing
Take up the sts from the first stitch holder. Join yarn
   and pick up and knit 3 sts along bottom of
   thumb; then take up and knit the sts from the
   second stitch holder.
Row 14: P20 {23, 26}, k2, p2, k2, p2, k2, p3 {4, 5}.
Row 15: K3 {4, 5}, p2, LT, p2, LT, p2, k20 {23, 26}.
Repeat rows 14 and 15 until mitten measures 3
   {3½, 4} inches above the cuff.
Small and medium size, skip to decrease row 1;
   large size decrease once first, as follows:

Hand

Row 1: K19 {22, 25}, p2, LT, p2, LT, p2, k3 {4, 5}.

Row 2: P3 {4, 5}, k2, p2, k2, p2, k2, p19 {22, 25}.

Rows 3–4: Repeat rows 1–2.

Row 5: K14 {16, 18}, kfb in each of next 2 sts, k3 {4, 5}, p2, LT, p2, LT, p2, k3 {4, 5}.

Row 6: P3, k2, p2, k2, p2, k2, p21 {24, 27}.

Row 7: K14 {16, 18}, kfb, k2, kfb, k3 {4, 5}, p2, LT, p2, LT, p2, k3 {4, 5}.

Row 8: P3, k2, p2, k2, p2, k2, p23 {26, 29}.

Row 9: K14 {16, 18}, kfb, k4, kfb, k3 {4, 5}, p2, LT, p2, LT, p2, k3 {4, 5}.

Row 10: P3, k2, p2, k2, p2, k2, p25 {28, 31}.

Row 11: K14 {16, 18}, kfb, k6, kfb, k3 {4, 5}, p2, LT, p2, LT, p2, k3 {4, 5}.

Row 12: P3, k2, p2, k2, p2, k2, p27 {30, 33}.

Small and medium size, go to row 13; large size increase once more as follows:

Final increase row **(large size only)**: K18, kfb, k8, kfb, k5, p2, LT, p2, LT, p2, k5.

Next row: P5, k2, p2, k2, p2, k2, p35. Now go to row 13.

Row 13: K14 {16, 18}; slip these sts to a stitch holder. Knit next 10 {10, 12} sts; slip rem 16 {18, 20} sts to a second stitch holder.

Thumb

Work as for right mitten.

Hand Finishing

Take up the sts from the first stitch holder. Join yarn and pick up and knit 3 sts along bottom of thumb; then take up the sts from the second stitch holder and work as follows: k3 {4, 5}, p2, LT, p2, LT, p2, k3 {4, 5}.

Row 14: P3 {4, 5}, k2, p2, k2, p2, k2, p20 {23, 26}.

Row 15: K20 {23, 26}, p2, LT, p2, LT, p2, k3 {4, 5}.

Repeat rows 14 and 15 until mitten measures 3 {3 1/2, 4} inches above the cuff.

Finish as for right mitten.

Decrease row 0 **(large size only)**: K1, *k8, k2tog; repeat from * to end.

Next row: Purl.

Decrease row 1 **(small and medium start here)**: K3, *k4, k2tog; repeat from * to end.

Next row: Purl.

Decrease row 2: K3, *k3, k2tog; repeat from * to end.

Next row: Purl.

Decrease row 3: K3, *k2, k2tog; repeat from * to end.

Next row: Purl.

Decrease row 4: *K1, k2tog; repeat from * to end.

Next row: Purl.

Last row: *K2tog across.

Break yarn, draw end through rem sts, and fasten off. Sew side seam and weave in ends.

LEFT MITTEN

Work as for right mitten to hand.

Garden Party Gloves

Lightweight and decorated with a lace panel, these gloves are a great accessory for a chilly spring day. The cotton yarn has very little stretch, so check your gauge carefully to be sure they'll fit.

YARN
Cascade Yarns Ultra Pima (100% Pima cotton, 220 yd/200 m; 3.5 oz/100 g) in periwinkle (1 skein)

NEEDLES
1 set size 3/3.25 mm double-pointed needles
or size needed to obtain gauge

NOTIONS
Stitch markers
Scrap yarn

MEASUREMENTS
7" long

GAUGE
7 stitches / 9 rounds = 1"

PATTERN

LEFT GLOVE

Cuff

Cast on 70 sts.

Round 1: Knit.

Round 2: *K1, k2tog, yo twice, k2tog, repeat from* around.

Round 3: Knit, dropping the second loop of each yo twice as you go.

Round 4: *K1, yo twice, k2tog, k1, repeat from* around.

Rounds 5–18: Repeat rounds 3 and 4.

Rounds 19–22: Knit.

Round 23: *K1, k2tog, k1, repeat from* around.

Rounds 24–26: Knit.

Hand

Lace panel (worked over the first 13 sts of each round):

Round A: K2, k2tog, yo, k2, yo, k2tog, k1, yo, ssk, k2.

Round B: Knit.

Round C: K1, k2tog, yo, k3, yo, k2tog, k2, yo, ssk, k1.

Round D: Knit.

Round E: K2tog, yo, k4, yo, k2tog, k3, yo, ssk.

Round F: Knit.

Round G: K6, yo, k2tog, k9.

Round H: Knit.

(These 8 rounds are repeated a total of 4 times for the hand of each glove.)

Round 27: [Work panel], k to end of round.

> The only difference in the hand between right and left gloves is round 28, where the stitch markers for the thumb increase are placed. Work the appropriate version of round 28 for each hand, then continue as given for each glove.

Round 28 (left mitten): [Work panel], k until last 5 sts, place stitch marker, kfb, place stitch marker, k to end of round.

Round 28 (right mitten): [Work panel], k4, place stitch marker, kfb, place stitch marker, k to end of round.

Rounds 29 (both mittens): [Work panel], k to end of round.

Round 30: Repeat round 29.

Round 31: [Work panel], k to marker, kfb, kfb, k to end of round.

Rounds 32–33: Repeat round 29.

Round 34: [Work panel], k to marker, kfb, k to one st before second marker, kfb, k to end of round.

Repeat rounds 32–34 until there are 12 sts between markers, ending with a round 33.

Next round: [Work panel], k to marker, place sts between markers on stitch holder or piece of scrap yarn, cast on 1, k to end.

Continue to work in pattern, working the panel first on each round, then knitting to the end of the round, until you have repeated panel rounds A–H a total of 4 times (ending on round H). End of lace panel.

Knit 3 rounds even.

First Finger

Knit first 2 sts; slip next 29 sts to a piece of scrap yarn; cast on 2 sts, knit rem 11 sts. Divide these 15 sts evenly on 3 needles and knit 5 more rounds even. Bind off loosely.

on 3 needles and knit in the round for 5 rounds. Bind off loosely.

Weave in all ends and block the gloves.

RIGHT GLOVE

Work as for left glove to fingers.

Fourth Finger

Knit first 2 sts; slip next 33 sts to a piece of scrap yarn; cast on 2 sts; knit rem 7 sts. Divide these 11 sts on 3 needles and knit 5 more rounds even. Bind off loosely.

Third Finger

Take up and knit 5 sts from the palm end of the piece of scrap yarn; cast on 2 sts; take up and knit 5 sts from the back end of the scrap yarn (the side of the glove with the lace pattern); pick up and knit 2 sts on the cast-on sts from the previous finger. Divide these 14 sts on 3 needles and knit 5 more rounds even. Bind off loosely.

Second Finger

Same as third finger.

First Finger

Take up and knit rem 13 sts from scrap yarn; pick up and knit 2 sts along the cast-on sts from the previous finger. Divide these 15 sts evenly on 3 needles and knit 5 more rounds even. Bind off loosely.

Thumb

Work as for left glove.

Second Finger

Take up and knit 5 sts from the back end of the scrap yarn (the side with the lace pattern); cast on 2 sts; take up and knit 5 sts from the palm end; pick up and knit 2 sts on the cast-on sts from the previous finger. Divide these 14 sts on 3 needles and knit 5 more rounds even. Bind off loosely.

Third Finger

Same as second finger.

Fourth Finger

Take up and knit rem 9 sts from scrap yarn; pick up and knit 2 sts along the cast-on sts from the previous finger. Divide these 11 sts evenly on 3 needles and knit 5 more rounds even. Bind off loosely.

Thumb

Take up and knit 12 sts set aside for thumb; pick up and knit 5 stitches from the cast-on sts for the top edge of the thumb hole. Divide these 17 sts

Ice Cream Mittens

These mittens feature a long cuff to keep snow and cold air away from little wrists. In Neapolitan colors, as shown here, they are perfect for a little girl who loves pink; other children might prefer them in bright, contrasting colors, which will make the stripes on the cuffs really pop.

4

Medium

YARN
Loops & Threads Impeccable
(100% acrylic; 192 yd/175 m;
100 g/3.5 oz)
A: Neapolitan (1 skein)
B: soft rose (1 skein)

NEEDLES
1 set each size 3/3.25 mm and 8/5 mm
    straight needles *or size needed to obtain
    gauge*

NOTIONS
Scrap yarn

MEASUREMENTS
Small: 11½" long
Medium: 14" long
Large: 16¼" long

GAUGE
On size 3 needles, 5 sts / 7 rows = 1"

PATTERN

Instructions are for small size (6 years); instructions for medium (10 years) and large (12 years) are in brackets.

LEFT MITTEN

Cuff

With size 8 needles and color B, cast on 42 {45, 48} sts.

Ribbing row: *Yo, sl 1 st pwise, k2tog; repeat from * to end.

Work ribbing row 8 {10, 12} times total with B, then 4 {6, 8} times with A, 4 {6, 8} times with B, 4 {4, 4} times with A, 4 {4, 4} times with B, and 4 {8, 12} times with A. Break B.

Hand

Change to size 3 needles.

Row 1: With A, *p1, k2tog; repeat from * to end. (28 {30, 32} sts)

Row 2: *P1, k1; repeat from * to end.

Rows 3–8: Repeat row 2.

Row 9 (small): *K3, kfb; repeat from * to end. (35 sts)

Row 9 (medium): *K3, kfb; repeat from * to last 2 sts, k2. (37 sts)

Row 9 (large): *K4, kfb; repeat from * to last 2 sts, k2. (38 sts)

Row 10: Purl.

Row 11: Knit.

Repeat rows 10 and 11 three {four, five} more times.

Purl 1 row. (9 {11, 13} total rows stockinette st)

Dividing row: Knit first 11 {12, 12} sts. Knit next 6 {7, 8} sts with a piece of scrap yarn in a different color, then slip them back onto the left-hand needle and knit them again with regular yarn. Knit remaining 18 sts.

Work even in stockinette st for 19 {19, 21} rows.

Small size: Go to dec row 1.

Next row (medium): K17, k2tog, k to end.

Next row (large): K1, k2tog, k16, k2tog, k to end.

Work 3 rows even (medium and large only).

Dec row 1 (all sizes): K5 {k0, k0}, *k2tog, k4; repeat from * to end. (30 {30, 30} sts)

Next row: Purl.
Dec row 2: *K2tog, k3; repeat from * to end.
Next row: Purl.
Dec row 3: *K2tog, k2; repeat from * to end.
Next row: Purl.
Dec row 4: *K2tog, k1; repeat from * to end.
Next row: Purl.
Last row: K2tog across.
Break yarn, draw end through rem sts, and fasten off.

Thumb

Pull out the colored yarn that the thumb sts were knitten onto, and slip the sts along the top of the opening to a strand of yarn and the sts along the bottom of the opening to a size 3 needle.

With A, cast on 3 {4, 4} sts to a free needle, knit the 6 {7, 8} thumb sts, then cast on 3 {3, 4} more sts. (12 {14, 16} sts)

Work in stockinette st for 9 {11, 13} rows.
Next row: K2tog across.
Break yarn, draw end through rem sts.

RIGHT MITTEN

Work as for left mitten up to dividing row.
Dividing row: Knit first 18 sts. Knit next 6 {7, 8} sts with a piece of scrap yarn in a different color, then slip them back onto the left-hand needle and knit them again with regular yarn. Knit remaining 11 {12, 12} sts.
Finish as for left mitten.

FINISHING

Sew side seam of thumb; weave the cast-on sts of the thumb to the sts on the strand of yarn, with the thumb seam at the center. Sew side seam of mitten.

Midwinter Mittens

You can't get much warmer than these thick, cozy mittens! Made with extra bulky yarn in a soft wool-acrylic blend, they are fast to make, even with the cables.

Super Bulky

YARN
Loops & Threads Cozy Wool
(50% wool, 50% acrylic;
90 yd/82 m; 4.5 oz/127 g)
in thunder (1 skein)

NEEDLES
1 set size 10/6 mm straight needles *or size
needed to obtain gauge*

NOTIONS
Cable needle
Stitch holders or scrap yarn (2)

MEASUREMENTS
10³/₄" long

GAUGE
6 sts / 9 rows = 2"

SPECIAL STITCH
Cable 6 front (C6F): Slip next 3 sts to a cable
needle, hold in front of work; knit next 3
sts, then knit the 3 sts from the cable
needle.

PATTERN

RIGHT MITTEN

Hand

Cast on 26 sts.

Row 1 (WS): P14, k2, p6, k2, p2.
Row 2 (RS): K2, p2, C6F, p2, k14.
Row 3: Repeat row 1.
Row 4: K2, p2, k6, p2, k14.
Row 5: Repeat row 1.
Row 6: Repeat row 4.
Rows 7–15: Repeat rows 1–6, ending with a row 3.
Row 16: K2, p2, k6, p2, k2, M1, k1, M1, k11.
Row 17: P16, k2, p6, k2, p2.
Row 18: K2, p2, k6, p2, k2, M1, k3, M1, k11.
Row 19: P18, k2, p6, k2, p2.
Row 20: K2, p2, C6F, p2, k2, M1, k5, M1, k11.
Row 21: P20, k2, p6, k2, p2.
Row 22: K2, p2, k6, p2, k2, M1, k7, M1, k11.
Row 23: P22, k2, p6, k2, p2.
Row 24: K2, p2, k6, p2, k2; slip these sts to a stitch holder or piece of scrap yarn. Knit next 9 sts (thumb); slip rem 11 sts to a stitch holder.

Thumb

Cast on 1 st at end of 9 thumb sts; work even in stockinette st on these 10 sts for 2¼ inches, ending with a purl row.
Last row: K2tog across.
Break yarn, draw end through rem sts, and fasten off. Sew thumb seam.

Hand Finishing

Take up the 14 sts from first stitch holder. Join yarn and pick up and knit 3 sts on stitch cast on for thumb; take up and knit the 11 sts from second stitch holder. (28 sts)
Row 25: P16, k2, p6, k2, p2.
Row 26: K2, p2, C6F, p2, k16.
Row 27: Repeat row 25.

Row 28: K2, p2, k6, p2, k16.
Row 29: Repeat row 25.
Row 30: Repeat row 28.
Rows 31–39: Repeat rows 25–30, ending with a row 27.

For a longer mitten, repeat rows 25–30 once more (ending with row 45, one row after a cable row).

Row 40: K2, p2tog, k6, p2tog, k4, k2tog, k6, ssk, k2. (24 sts)
Row 41: P14, k1, p6, k1, p2.
Row 42: K2, k2tog, k4, ssk, k4, k2tog, k4, ssk, k2. (20 sts)
Row 43: Purl.
Row 44: K2tog across.
Break yarn, draw end through rem sts, and fasten off. Sew side seam and weave in ends.

LEFT MITTEN
Hand
Cast on 26 sts.
Row 1 (WS): P2, k2, p6, k2, p14.
Row 2 (RS): K14, p2, C6F, p2, k2.
Row 3: Repeat row 1.
Row 4: K14, p2, k6, p2, k2.
Row 5: Repeat row 1
Row 6: Repeat row 4.
Rows 7–15: Repeat rows 1–6, ending with a row 3.
Row 16: K11, M1, k1, M1, k2, p2, k6, p2, k2.
Row 17: P2, k2, p6, k2, p16.
Row 18: K11, M1, k3, M1, k2, p2, k6, p2, k2.
Row 19: P2, k2, p6, k2, p18.
Row 20: K11, M1, k5, M1, k2, p2, k6, p2, k2.
Row 21: P2, k2, p6, k2, p20.
Row 22: K11, M1, k7, M1, k2, p2, k6, p2, k2.
Row 23: P2, k2, p6, k2, p22.
Row 24: K11; slip these sts to a stitch holder or piece of scrap yarn. Knit next 9 sts (thumb); slip rem 14 sts to a stitch holder.

Thumb
Work as for right mitten.

Hand Finishing
Take up the 11 sts from first stitch holder. Join yarn and pick up and knit 3 sts on stitch cast on for thumb; take up and knit the 14 sts from second stitch holder as follows: k2, p2, k6, p2, k2. (28 sts)
Row 25: P2, k2, p6, k2, p16.
Row 26: K16, p2, C6F, p2, k2.
Row 27: Repeat row 25.
Row 28: K16, p2, k6, p2, k2.
Row 29: Repeat row 25.
Row 30: Repeat row 28.
Rows 31–39: Repeat rows 25–30, ending with a row 27.

For a longer mitten, repeat rows 25–30 once more (ending with row 45, one row after a cable row).

Row 40: K2, k2tog, k6, ssk, k4, p2tog, k6, p2tog, k2. (24 sts)
Row 41: P2, k1, p6, k1, p14.
Finish as for right mitten.

Oslo Mittens

These soft Nordic-style mittens are similar to the frostrosen mittens on page 22, but are made in a lighter weight yarn that allows a more intricate design. Since the whole project, except for the cuff and thumb, is knitted alternating between two strands of yarn, these mittens are extra thick and warm, even with the lighter yarn.

2

Fine

YARN
Knit Picks Stroll Sport (75%
superwash merino wool, 25%
nylon; 137 yd; 50 g) in
A: fedora (1 skein)
B: mink heather (1 skein)

NEEDLES
1 set size 1/2.25 mm double-pointed needles
or size needed to obtain gauge

NOTIONS
Stitch holder or scrap yarn

MEASUREMENTS
11" long

GAUGE
8 sts / 9 rounds = 1"

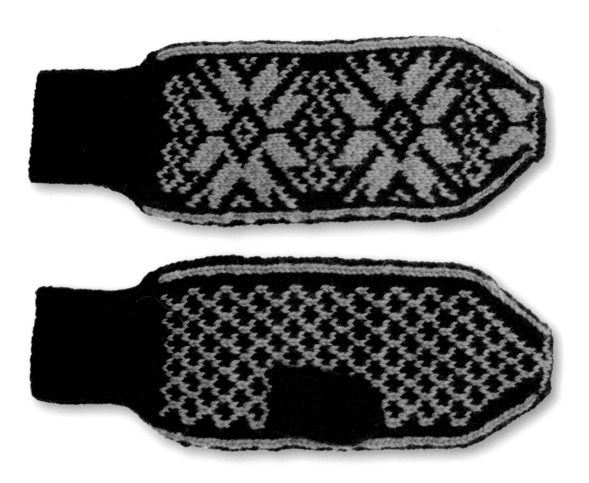

PATTERN

RIGHT MITTEN
Cuff
With color A, cast on 50 sts (25 on first needle, 11 on second, 14 on third). Join to work in round.
Work k1, p1 ribbing around for 3 inches.
Increase round: K2, *inc in next st, k5; repeat from * around. (58 sts)

Hand
Follow the chart on page 62, working in stockinette stitch, for 21 rows.
Row 22: Work first 33 sts as on chart. Knit next 9 sts onto a piece of scrap yarn (for the thumb), then slip them back onto the left-hand needle and knit them again in the pattern. Continue following chart to end of round.
Continue in pattern until the end of the 56th round.
Round 57: K1 in A, k1 in B, k2tog in A, k3 in A; continue in pattern to last 4 sts on first needle; with A, ssk, k1 in B, k1 in A. K1 in A (first st on second needle), k1 in B, k2tog in A, k3 in A; follow chart to last 4 sts on third needle; ssk in A, k1 in B, k1 in A.
Round 58: Work even, following chart.
Round 59: K1 in A, k1 in B; k2tog in A, k1 in B; follow chart to last 4 sts on first needle; ssk in A, k1 in B, k1 in A. K1 in A, k1 in B, k2tog in A, k2 in A; follow chart to last 4 sts on third needle; ssk in A, k1 in B, k1 in A.
Continue to decrease in this pattern, working the first and second stitch on each side of the mitten even and working the third and fourth stitches together (and doing the same on the other side, i.e. working the last two stitches even and working the third and fourth stitches from the end of the side together). Follow the chart for the decreases: Decrease 4 sts every other row 4 more times, then decrease 4 sts in every row up to the last row of the chart. (22 sts at end of second-to-last row)
Break B. Knit the 11 sts of the back with A; break A, leaving a long tail. Weave the sts from the back and palm together.

Thumb
Pull out the scrap yarn that the 9 thumb sts were knitted onto. Pick up 9 sts on the top and bottom of this opening and divide them onto 3 needles. Join color A and knit around the thumb, picking up and knitting one more stitch on each end of the opening. (20 sts)
Knit around even for 2¼ inches.

Dec round 1: *K2, k2tog; repeat from * around.
   (15 sts)
Knit 1 round even.
Dec round 2: *K1, k2tog; repeat from * around.
   (10 sts)
Knit 1 round even.
Break yarn, draw end through rem sts, and fasten
   off. Weave in ends.

LEFT MITTEN
Work as for right mitten until round 22.
Round 22: Work first 45 sts as on chart. Knit next 9
   sts onto a piece of scrap yarn (for the thumb),
   then slip them back onto the left-hand needle
   and knit them again in the pattern. Continue
   following chart to end of round.
Finish as for right mitten.

■ = Color A

▨ = Color B

Checkerboard Mittens

SKILL LEVEL

EXPERIENCED

These colorful mittens with a Fair-Isle checkerboard pattern are a great project for a knitter who loves to play with color. They may look complicated, but you are never using more than two colors in any one row.

YARN
Knit Picks Palette (100% Peruvian highland wool; 231 yd; 50 g) in

Lace

A: delta (1 skein)
B: cornmeal (1 skein)
C: masala (1 skein)
D: sky (1 skein)
E: edamame (1 skein)
F: silver (1 skein)

NEEDLES
1 set size 2/2.75 mm double-pointed needles
or size needed to obtain gauge

NOTIONS
Scrap yarn

MEASUREMENTS
11" long

GAUGE
Fair Isle pattern: 8 sts / 9 rows = 1"

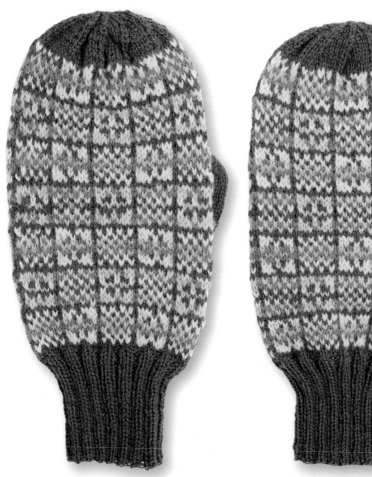

PATTERN

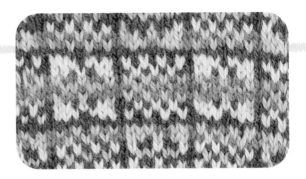

RIGHT MITTEN

Cuff

With A, cast on 64 sts; divide on 3 needles; join, taking care not to twist sts on needles. Work k 2, p 2 ribbing for 3 ins.

Increase round: *K 3, kfb; repeat from * around. (80 sts)

Hand

Knit all sts on each row, working in Fair Isle pattern from chart on page 66. Carry the yarn not in use on wrong side of work.

Repeat the 16 rounds of the pattern until about 2 1/2 inches above cuff.

Thumb round: Work pattern on first 42 sts; with a separate strand of colored yarn, k next 12 sts for thumb, then slip these sts back to left-hand needle and continue pattern.

Continue to work in pattern until about 7 inches above cuff, ending with 8th or 16th pattern round. Break off all colors except A.

With A, k 1 round even.

First dec. round: *K6, k2tog; repeat from * around. (70 sts)

Knit 1 round even.

Second dec. round: *K5, k2tog; repeat from * around. (60 sts)

Knit 1 round even.

Third dec. round: *K4, k2tog; repeat from * around. (50 sts)

Knit 1 round even.

Fourth dec. round: *K3, k2tog; repeat from * around. (40 sts)

Knit 1 round even.

Fifth dec. round: *K2, k2tog; repeat from * around. (30 sts)

Knit 1 round even.

Sixth dec. round: *K1, k2tog; repeat from * around. (20 sts)

Knit 1 round even.

Last round: K2tog 10 times. (10 sts)

Break off yarn; draw end through all 10 sts. Fasten off.

Thumb

Draw out colored yarn; pick up these 12 sts. Pick up 1 st on either side of the opening and 12 more sts along top edge of opening. Divide these 26 sts on 3 needles. With A only, k around for 2 1/4 inches.

Next round: *K 11, k2tog; repeat from * around. (24 sts)

First decrease round: *K 2, k2tog; repeat from *
  around. (18 sts)
K 1 round even.
Second decrease round: *K 1, k2tog; repeat from *
  around. (12 sts)
K 1 round even.
Last round: K2tog 6 times. (6 sts)
Break off yarn; draw end through all 10 sts. Fasten
  off.
Weave in all ends.

LEFT MITTEN
Work same as right mitten until thumb round.
Thumb round: Work pattern on first 26 sts; with a
  separate strand of colored yarn, k next 12 sts for
  thumb, then slip these sts back to left-hand
  needle and continue pattern.
Finish as for right mitten.

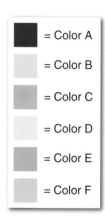

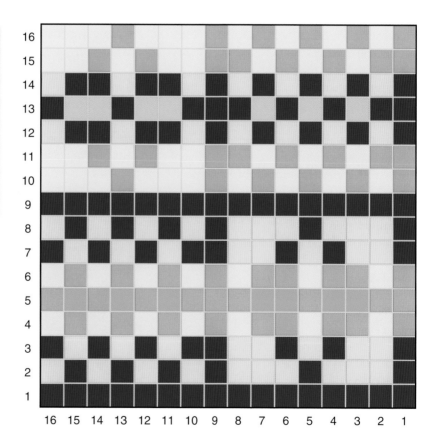

Icicle Mittens

SKILL LEVEL

INTERMEDIATE

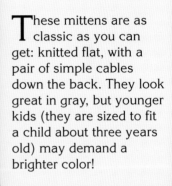

These mittens are as classic as you can get: knitted flat, with a pair of simple cables down the back. They look great in gray, but younger kids (they are sized to fit a child about three years old) may demand a brighter color!

Medium

YARN
Red Heart Super Soft (100% acrylic; 515 yd/471 m; 10 oz/ 283 g) in heather gray (1 skein)

NEEDLES
1 set size 3/3.25 mm straight needles *or size needed to obtain gauge*

NOTIONS
Cable needle
Stitch holders or scrap yarn (2)

MEASUREMENTS
6¹/₂" long

GAUGE
4 sts / 7 rows = 1"

SPECIAL STITCH
Cable 4 back (C4B): Slip 2 sts to a cable needle and hold in back of work. Knit the next 2 sts, then knit the 2 sts from the cable needle.

PATTERN

RIGHT MITTEN
Cuff
Cast on 32 sts.
Work in k1, p1 ribbing for 2¼ inches.

Thumb Gusset
Row 1: K2, p1, [k4, p1] twice, k19.
Row 2: P19, [k1, p4] twice, k1, p2.
Row 3: K2, p1, [C4B, p1] twice, k19.
Row 4: Repeat row 2.
Row 5: K2, p1, [k4, p1] twice, k2, kfb, k1, kfb, k14.
Row 6: P21, [k1, p4] twice, k1, p2.
Row 7: K2, p1, [k4, p1] twice, k2, kfb, k3, kfb, k14.
Row 8: P23, [k1, p4] twice, k1, p2.
Row 9: K2, p1, [C4B, p1] twice, k2, kfb, k5, kfb, k14.
Row 10: P25, [k2, p4] twice, k1, p2.
Row 11: K2, p1, [k4, p1] twice, k25.
Row 12: Repeat row 10.
Row 13: K2, p1, [k4, p1] twice, k2; place these sts on a stitch holder or piece of scrap yarn. Knit next 9 sts; leave on needle. Place rem 14 sts on a second stitch holder.

Thumb
Cast on 1 st at end of 9 sts. Turn and purl back; cast on 1 st at other end. Work these 11 sts in stockinette st until thumb measures 1¼ inches, ending on a purl row.
Next row: K2tog across.
Break yarn, draw end through rem sts, and fasten off. Sew thumb seam.

Hand
Take up the sts from the first stitch holder. Join yarn and pick up and knit 4 sts along the bottom of the thumb. Take up and knit the sts from the second stitch holder.
Row 14: P20, [k1, p4] twice, k1, p2.
Row 15: K2, p1, [C4B, p1] twice, k20.
Row 16: Repeat row 14.
Row 17: K2, p1, [k4, p1] twice, k20.
Row 18: Repeat row 14.
Row 19: Repeat row 17.
Repeat rows 14–19 until mitten measures 3 inches from the end of the ribbing.

Finishing
Dec row 1: *K4, k2tog; repeat from * across.
Next row: Purl.
Dec row 2: *K3, k2tog; repeat from * across.
Next row: Purl.
Dec row 3: *K2, k2tog; repeat from * across.
Next row: Purl.
Dec row 4: *K1, k2tog; repeat from * across.

Last row: P2tog across.
Break yarn, pull end through rem sts, and fasten off. Sew side seam and weave in ends.

LEFT MITTEN
Work cuff as for right mitten.

Thumb Gusset
Row 1: K19, [p1, k4] twice, p1, k2.
Row 2: P2, k1, [p4, k1] twice, p19.
Row 3: K19, [p1, C4B] twice, p1, k2.
Row 4: Repeat row 2.
Row 5: K14, kfb, k1, kfb, k2, [p1, k4] twice, p1, k2.
Row 6: P2, k1, [p4, k1] twice, p21.
Row 7: K14, kfb, k3, kfb, k2, [p1, k4] twice, p1, k2.
Row 8: P2, k1, [p4, k1] twice, p23.
Row 9: K14, kfb, k5, kfb, k2, [p1, C4B] twice, p1, k2.
Row 10: P2, k1, [p4, k1] twice, p25.
Row 11: K25, [p1, k4] twice, p1, k2.
Row 12: P2, k1, [p4, k1] twice, p25.
Row 13: K14; place these sts on a stitch holder or piece of scrap yarn. Knit next 9 sts; leave on needle. Place rem 15 sts on a second stitch holder.

Thumb
Work as for right mitten.

Hand
Take up the sts from the first stitch holder. Join yarn and pick up and knit 4 sts along the bottom of the thumb. Take up and work the sts from the second stitch holder as follows: k2, [p1, k4] twice, p1, k2.
Row 14: P2, k1, [p4, k1] twice, p20.

Row 15: K20, [p1, C4B] twice, p1, k2.
Row 16: Repeat row 14.
Row 17: K20, [p1, k4] twice, p1, k2.
Row 18: Repeat row 14.
Row 19: Repeat row 17.
Repeat rows 14–19 until mitten measures 3 inches from the end of the ribbing.
Finish as for right mitten.

Raspberry Sorbet Gloves

SKILL LEVEL

INTERMEDIATE

These lacy gloves are made with 100% wool yarn, but are still light enough to be suitable for spring or fall. Work the first few rows flat on two double-pointed needles for the scalloped cuff edging, then cast on the stitches for the inside of the wrist and work the rest of the gloves in the round.

1
Super Fine

YARN
Jojoland Ballad (100%
superwash wool; 220 yd; 50g)
in grape (2 skeins)

NEEDLES
1 set size 1/2.25 mm double-pointed needles
or size needed to obtain gauge

MEASUREMENTS
10½" long

GAUGE
9 sts / 11 rnds = 1" (in stockinette stitch)

PATTERN

RIGHT GLOVE
Cuff
Cast on 28 sts for hem of back of glove.

Row 1: Purl.

Row 2: Knit.

Rows 3–4: Repeat rows 1–2.

Row 5 (WS): K1, *yo, k2tog; repeat from * to last st, k1 in last st.

Row 6: Knit across. Cast on 30 sts at end of row. (58 sts) Divide these 58 sts onto three needles (28 sts on first needle, 12 sts on second needle, 16 sts on third needle); join to work in round.

Hand
First round: K28, p2, *k2, p2; repeat from * to end of round.

Repeat this round 2 more times.

Begin lace pattern:

Round 1: K3, *yo, ssk, k2, k2tog, yo, k2; repeat from * twice; k1; work p2, k2 ribbing to end of round.

Round 2: K28, work ribbing to end.

Round 3: K4, *yo, ssk, k2tog, yo, k4; repeat from * twice; work ribbing to end.

Round 4: Repeat round 2.

Repeat pattern until ribbing measures 2 inches, decreasing 2 sts in ribbing on last round. (56 sts)

First increase round for thumb gusset: Work pattern for 28 sts, place a marker before next st, k1, M1, k1, M1, k1, place a marker before next st (5 sts in thumb gusset), k to end of round. (58 sts)

Work 3 rounds even, with first 28 sts in pattern and rem sts in stockinette st. Carry the thumb markers up as you go.

Second increase round: Work to first marker, k1, M1, k3, M1, k1, k to end of round.

Continue in this pattern, increasing 2 sts in the thumb on every fourth round, having 2 more sts between the M1s in each increase round, until there are 21 sts between the markers. (74 sts in last increase round)

Work 2 rounds even.

Next round: Work 28 pattern sts; slip next 21 sts to a stitch holder or strand of scrap yarn for the thumb. Onto a free needle, cast on 7 sts for side of hand, then knit rem sts from 2nd needle onto this needle; k to end of round. (60 sts)

Work 1½ inches even, working the pattern on the back of the hand and stockinette st on the palm, ending just before the 7 cast-on sts with pattern round 4. This completes the lace portion.

First Finger
Slip last 7 sts worked to a free needle; to the same needle, k next 10 sts (the sts right over the 7 cast-on sts, plus the next 3 sts). Slip the rem 43 sts to a piece of scrap yarn to be held for the rest of the fingers. Cast on 5 sts for the gusset.

Divide these 22 sts on 3 needles; join to work in round. Knit even for 2½ inches, or ¼ inch less than desired length.

Dec round 1: K9, k2tog, k9, k2tog. (20 sts)

Knit 1 round even.

Dec round 2: *K3, k2tog; repeat from * to end of round. (16 sts)

Knit 1 round even.

Dec round 3: *K2, k2tog; repeat from * to end of round. (12 sts)

Knit 1 round even.

Last round: K2tog all round. (6 sts)

Break yarn, draw through rem sts, pull tight, and fasten off.

Second Finger

Beginning at back of hand (lace section), slip 8 sts from scrap yarn to needle. Join yarn and pick up and knit 5 sts on cast-on sts from first finger. Slip 7 sts from other end of scrap yarn onto a free needle and knit them. Cast on 4 sts for gusset.

Divide these 24 sts onto 3 needles; join to work in round. Knit even for 2¾ inches, or ¼ inch less than desired length.

Dec round 1: *K4, k2tog; repeat from * to end of round. (20 sts)

Knit 1 round even.

Finish as for first finger, starting with dec round 1.

Third Finger

Slip 7 sts from back of hand to needle; pick up and knit 4 sts on cast-on sts from second finger; knit 7 sts from palm of hand; cast on 4 sts for gusset.

Divide these 22 sts on 3 needles; join to work in round. Knit even for 2½ inches, or ¼ inch less than desired length.

Finish as for first finger.

Fourth Finger

Slip rem 14 sts to 2 needles; pick up and knit 4 sts on cast-on sts from third finger. Divide these 18 sts on 3 needles; join to work in round. Knit even for 2 inches, or ¼ inch less than desired length.

First dec round: K7, k2tog, k7, k2tog. (16 sts)

Knit 1 round even.

Finish as for first finger, starting with dec round 3.

Thumb

Slip the 21 thumb sts to 2 needles; pick up and knit 7 sts on cast-on sts for side of hand. Divide these 28 sts onto 3 needles; join to work in round. Knit 3 rounds even.

†Dec round: Dec 1 st in center of 7 picked-up sts. Knit 1 round even.†

Repeat between the †s 3 more times. (24 sts)

Knit even until 2 inches above picked-up sts, or ¼ inch less than desired length.

Finish as for second finger.

LEFT GLOVE

Work same as right glove until first increase round for thumb gusset.

First increase round for thumb gusset: Work pattern for 28 sts, k to last 3 sts of round, place a marker before next st, k1, M1, k1, M1, k1, place another marker (5 sts in thumb gusset). (58 sts)

Work 3 rounds even, with first 28 sts in pattern and rem sts in stockinette st. Carry the thumb markers up as you go.

Second increase round: Work to first marker, k1, M1, k3, M1, k1.

Continue in this pattern, as for the right glove, increasing 2 sts in the thumb on every fourth round, having 2 more sts between the M1s in each increase round, until there are 21 sts between the markers. (74 sts in last increase round)

Work 2 rounds even.

Next round: Work 28 pattern sts; k to first marker; slip next 21 sts to a stitch holder or strand of scrap yarn for the thumb; cast on 7 sts; join. (60 sts)

Work 1½ inches even, working the pattern on the back of the hand and stockinette st on the palm, ending with pattern round 4, at the end of the round (just after the 7 cast-on sts). This completes the lace portion.

First Finger

Slip the last 10 sts worked to a free needle (the sts right over the cast-on sts and the previous 3 sts); to the same needle knit the next 7 sts. Slip rem 43 sts to a strand of scrap yarn. Cast on 5 sts for gusset.

Divide these 22 sts on 3 needles; join.

Finish as for first finger of right glove.

Finish remaining fingers to correspond to right glove.

FINISHING

Turn under bottom edge of cuff along back of hand to form a scalloped border; sew in place. Weave in all ends.

Block the gloves to even out the lace and help it look its best.

Peach Blossom Baby Mittens

SKILL LEVEL

EASY

Knitted flat in one piece, with no thumb, these adorable baby mittens are the quickest and easiest project in this book. Make them in lightweight cotton yarn for a summer baby or in soft baby wool for a winter arrival.

3
Light

YARN
Cotton sport or baby yarn in peach (1 skein)

NEEDLES
1 set size 4/3.5 mm straight needles *or size needed to obtain gauge*

NOTIONS
Ribbon
Sewing needle
Sewing thread

MEASUREMENTS
4" long

GAUGE
5 sts / 9 rows = 1"

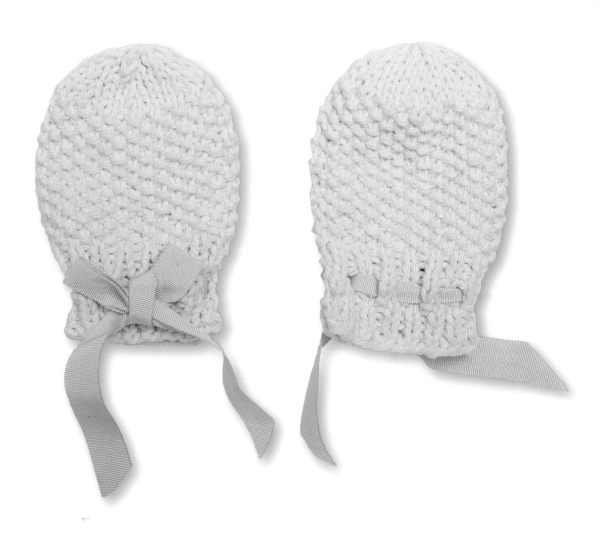

PATTERN

Cuff

Cast on 29 sts.

Row 1 (WS): *K1, p1; repeat from * to last st, k1.

Row 2 (RS): *P1, k1; repeat from * to last st, p1.

Row 3: Repeat row 1.

Row 4: Repeat row 2.

Row 5: Repeat row 1.

Row 6 [eyelet row]: *K2tog, yo; repeat from * to last
     st, k1.

Rows 7–11: Repeat rows 1–5.

Hand

Row 12: Repeat row 1.

Continue to work row 1 until piece measures 2 1/2
     inches above the ribbing. End with a WS row.

Dec row 1: K1, *k2tog, k3; repeat from * across.

Purl 1 row.

Dec row 2: K1, *k2tog, k2; repeat from * across.

Purl 1 row.

Dec row 3: K1, *k2tog, k1; repeat from * across.

Final dec row: P2tog across.

Break yarn, draw end through rem sts, fasten off.
     Sew side seam and weave in ends.

Make another mitten exactly the same.

FINISHING

Thread a ribbon through the eyelet row, and tie it
     in a bow. If desired, tack down the bow with a
     few stitches through the center to keep it from
     coming untied.

Midnight Mittens

SKILL LEVEL

EASY

Worked mostly with two strands of 100% wool, worsted-weight yarn, these mittens are thick and warm. The wrist section is worked with smaller needles and only one strand of yarn, ensuring a snug fit at the wrist.

4

Medium

YARN
Cascade Yarns Cascade 220 Heathers (100% Peruvian highland wool; 220 yd/200 m; 3.5 oz/100 g) in mallard (2 skeins)

NEEDLES
1 set each size 3/3.25 mm and 8/5 mm straight needles *or size needed to obtain gauge*

NOTIONS
Yarn needle

MEASUREMENTS
12$\frac{1}{2}$" long

GAUGE
With size 8 needles and two strands of yarn, 4 sts / 3 rows = 1"

PATTERN

This pattern uses two strands of worsted-weight yarn for most of the mitten and one strand for the wrist. Divide your skein of yarn into two separate balls and use the yarn from both balls at once until you get to the wrist.

LEFT MITTEN

Cuff

With size 8 needles and two strands of yarn, cast on 48 sts.

Row 1 (WS): *K3, p1; repeat from * to end.

Row 2 (RS): *With yarn in back of work, sl 1 st kwise, p3; repeat from * to end.

Repeat rows 1 and 2 until work measures 3 inches; end with a RS row.

Dec row (WS): *K1, k2tog, p1; repeat from * to end. (36 sts)

Wrist

Break off 1 strand of yarn.

Next row (RS): With size 3 needles and 1 strand of yarn, *sl 1 st kwise, p2; repeat from * to end.

Next row (WS): *K2, p1; repeat from * to end.

Repeat these 2 rows for 1½ inches, ending with a RS row. Mark last row.

Hand

Join a second strand of yarn.

With size 8 needles and double strand of yarn, work pat:

Hand row 1 (WS): *K2, p1; repeat from * to end.

Hand row 2 (RS): *Sl 1 kwise, p2; repeat from * to end.

Repeat these 2 rows until 2 inches above marked row, ending on a WS row.

Thumb

Work 19 sts in pattern (row 1), cast on 5 sts on right-hand needle, turn. Work pattern (row 2— k2, p1) on the 5 cast-on sts and on next 7 sts, turn. Leave rem sts on needles.

Work even in pattern on 12 thumb sts until 2 inches from cast-on sts, ending on RS.

Dec row: *K2tog, p1; repeat from * to end. (8 sts)

Break off yarn, draw end tightly through rem thumb sts, and sew side seam of thumb.

Hand Finishing

Working from RS, join 2 strands of yarn in the 12th st of right-hand needle; pick up and k 7 sts across the 5 cast-on sts of the thumb. Continue in pattern to end. (36 sts)

Work even until 4 inches above picked-up sts or
within ½ inch of desired length, ending on RS.
Dec row 1: *K2tog, p1; repeat from * to end. (24 sts)
Next row: *Sl 1 st kwise, p1; repeat from * to end.
Dec row 2: K1, p2tog 11 times, p1. (13 sts)
Break off yarn, draw end tightly through rem sts,
and sew side seam. Weave in all ends.

RIGHT MITTEN

Work cuff, wrist, and hand same as left mitten until
2 inches above marker for beg of hand, ending
on WS.

Thumb

Work first 25 sts in pattern (row 1), cast on 5 sts on
right-hand needle, turn. Work pattern (row 2—
k2, p1) on the 5 cast-on sts and on next 7 sts,
turn. Leave rem sts on needles. Work thumb on
these 12 sts and finish as for left mitten. Break
yarn, fasten off, and sew seam.

Hand Finishing

Working from RS, join 2 strands of yarn in the 18th
st of the right-hand needle; pick up and knit 7
sts across the 5 cast-on sts of the thumb.
Continue in pattern to end. (36 sts)
Finish as for left mitten.

Annika Mittens

These colorful Nordic-style mittens are a great way to use up smaller amounts of colors left over from previous projects. Make them in whatever colors you have on hand—or let the recipient pick her own color scheme.

Medium

YARN
Knit Picks Bare Wool of the Andes (100% Peruvian Highland Wool; 110 yds; 50 g)
A: natural (1 skein)
Valley Yarns Northampton (100% wool, 247 yd; 100 g)
B: apple green (1 skein)
Plymouth Encore (75% acrylic, 25% wool; 200 yd; 3.5 oz/100 g)
C: red (1 skein)
D: yellow (1 skein)

NEEDLES
1 set size 3/3.25 mm double-pointed needles
or size needed to obtain gauge

NOTIONS
Scrap yarn

MEASUREMENTS
8¾" long

GAUGE
5 sts / 7 rnds = 1"

PATTERN

RIGHT MITTEN
Cuff
With A, cast on 36 sts. Divide on 3 needles; join to work in round, marking the end of the round. Work k2, p2 ribbing for 3 inches. Knit 2 rounds even.

Hand
Begin colorwork section as follows:

Round 1: *K1 with A, k2 with B; repeat from * around.

Round 2: *K1 with B, k2 with A; repeat from * around.

Continue to follow chart on page 86 until 10 rounds of pattern are completed.

Divide for thumb: With a strand of scrap yarn in a contrasting color, knit the first 6 sts. Slip these sts back to the left-hand needle and knit them again with regular yarn. Continue knitting to the end of the round.

Continue to follow chart until pattern is completed. Knit 2 rounds even with A.

Dec round 1: *K2, k2tog; repeat from * around. (27 sts)

Knit 2 rounds even.

Dec round 2: *K1, k2tog; repeat from * around. (18 sts)

Knit 1 round even.

Dec round 3: K2tog around. (9 sts)

Break yarn, leaving an end; draw the end through the rem sts and pull tightly. Fasten off.

Thumb
Pull out the strand of scrap yarn and pick up 6 sts on each side of the opening created; place these 12 sts on 3 needles. Join A in first st on upper needle.

From the right side, knit 1 round, picking up 1 st at inner edge of thumb at end of round. (13 sts)

Knit even for 2 inches, decreasing 1 st at end of last round. (12 sts)

Dec round: K2tog around. (6 sts)

Break yarn, draw end through rem sts, and fasten off.

Weave in all ends.

LEFT MITTEN

Work same as right mitten until 10 rounds of
    pattern are completed.

Divide for thumb: Knit around to last 6 sts of round.
    With a strand of scrap yarn in a contrasting
    color, knit these last 6 sts. Slip these sts back to
    the left-hand needle and knit them again with
    regular yarn.

Finish as for right mitten.

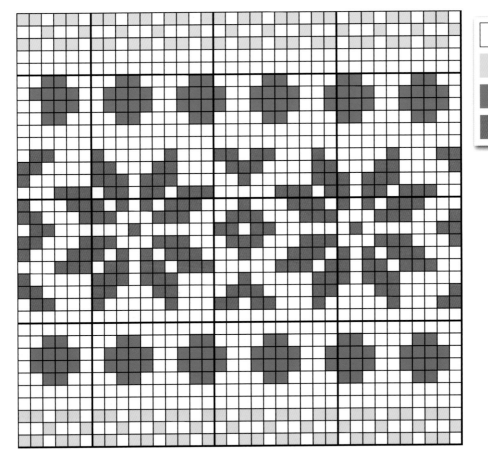

= Color A

= Color B

= Color C

= Color D

September Gloves

SKILL LEVEL

EASY

These soft, stylish gloves pair perfectly with a three-quarter-length-sleeve top for those spring and autum days that start out cold, warm up in the middle, and finish cold again. This is a good pattern for beginning knitters. The mock eyelet cable pattern keeps things interesting during the long section with no shaping, but with only four rows, it's simple enough to memorize.

3

Light

YARN
Cascade Yarns 220 Superwash
Sport (100% superwash merino
wool; 136 yd/125 m; 1.75 oz/
50 g), hand-dyed (2 skeins)

NEEDLES
1 set size 3/3.25 mm double-pointed needles
   or size needed to obtain gauge

NOTIONS
Stitch markers (2)

MEASUREMENTS
12½" long

GAUGE
In pattern, 8 sts / 8 rounds = 1"

PATTERN

RIGHT GLOVE
Cuff
Cast on 52 sts, divide on 3 needles, and join to work in round, being careful not to twist sts.

Begin pattern:

Round 1: *K2, p2; repeat from * to end.

Round 2: *K1, yo, k1, p2; repeat from * to end.

Round 3: *K3, p2; repeat from * to end.

Round 4: *Sl1, k2, psso, p2; repeat from * to end.

Repeat the 4 rounds of the pattern until the piece measures about 7½ inches, ending with a round 4.

Wrist
Dec round: [K2, p2tog] 6 times; work k2, p2 pattern to end. (42 sts)

Continue in pattern (starting with round 2), having only 1 purl st in the first 6 purl ribs, for 14 rounds (ending on a round 3).

Inc round: [Sl1, k2, psso, pfb in next st] 6 times; continue in normal round 4 pattern to end.

Hand
Hand round 1: Work 26 sts in pattern (round 1), place marker, pfb, p1, place another marker, continue in pattern to end of round. (3 sts between markers)

Rounds 2–3: Work in pattern to first marker, [p3] between markers, continue in pattern to end of round.

Round 4: Work in pattern (round 4) to first marker, [pfb, pfb, p1] between markers, continue in pattern to end of round. (5 sts between markers)

Round 5: Work in pattern to first marker, [p1, k2, p2] between markers, continue in pattern to end of round.

Round 6: Work in pattern to first marker, [p1, k1, yo, k1, p2] between markers, continue in pattern to end of round. (6 sts between markers)

Round 7: Work in pattern (round 3) to first marker, [pfb, k3, pfb, p1] between markers, continue in pattern to end of round. (8 sts between markers)

Round 8: Work in pattern to first marker, [p2, sl1, k2, psso, p3] between markers, continue in pattern to end of round. (7 sts between markers)

Round 9: Work in pattern to first marker, [p2, k2, p3] between markers, continue in pattern to end of round.

Round 10: Work in pattern (round 2) to first marker, [pfb, p1, k1, yo, k1, p1, pfb, p] between markers, continue in pattern to end of round. (10 sts between markers)

Round 11: Work in pattern to first marker, [p3, k3, p4] between markers, continue in pattern to end of round.

Round 12: Work in pattern to first marker, [p3, sl1, k2, psso, p4] between markers, continue in pattern to end of round. (9 sts between markers)

Round 13: Work in pattern (round 1) to first marker, [pfb, p2, k2, p2, pfb, p1] between markers, continue in pattern to end of round. (11 sts between markers)

Round 14: Work in pattern to first marker, [p1, yo, k1, p2, k1, yo, k1, p2, k1, yo, k1, p1] between markers, continue in pattern to end of round. (14 sts between markers)

Round 15: Work in pattern to first marker, [p1, k2, p2, k3, p2, k3, p1] between markers, continue in pattern to end of round.

Round 16: Work in pattern (round 4) to first marker, [pfb, sl1, k1, psso, p2, sl1, k2, psso, p2, sl1, k1, pfb, psso, p1] between markers, continue in pattern to end of round. (13 sts between markers)

Round 17: Work in pattern to first marker, [p1, (k2, p2) 3 times] between markers, continue in pattern to end of round.

Round 18: Work in pattern to first marker, [p1, (k1, yo, k1, p2) 3 times] between markers, continue in pattern to end of round. (16 sts between markers)

Round 19: Work in pattern (round 3) to first marker, [pfb, (k3, p2) twice, k3, pfb, p1] between markers, continue in pattern to end of round. (18 sts between markers)

Round 20: Work in pattern to first marker, [p2, (sl1, k2, psso, p2) 3 times, p1] between markers, continue in pattern to end of round. (15 sts between markers)

Round 21: Work in pattern (round 1) to first marker, purl all sts between markers, continue in pattern to end of round.

Round 22: Work in pattern to first marker, [(k2tog, yo) 7 times, k1] between markers, continue in pattern to end of round.

Round 23: Work in pattern to first marker, purl all sts between markers, continue in pattern to end of round.

Round 24: Work in pattern to first marker, p1, bind off 13 sts pwise, p1, continue in pattern to end of round.

Round 25: Work in pattern (round 1) to first marker, remove marker, p1, cast on 4, p1, remove second marker, continue in pattern to end of round.

Rounds 26–29: Work in pattern (ending on a round 1).

Round 30: Purl.

Round 31: *K2tog, yo; repeat from * to end.

Round 32: Purl.

Bind off pwise. Weave in ends.

LEFT GLOVE

Work as for right glove until wrist.

Wrist

Dec round: [K2, p2] 6 times; [K2, p2tog] 6 times. (42 sts)

Continue in pattern (starting with round 2), having only 1 purl st in the last 6 purl ribs, for 14 rounds (ending on a round 3).

Inc round: [Sl1, k2, psso, p2] 6 times; [Sl1, k2, psso, pfb in next st] 6 times.

Finish as for right glove.

Snowball Fight Mittens

SKILL LEVEL

INTERMEDIATE

For playing in the snow, long cuffs are a must. These mittens feature a good four inches of cuff on the smallest size, and the loose shaping of the cuff allows for it to be worn either pulled over the end of a coat sleeve or tucked inside. Be careful to cast on loosely to give the end of the cuff plenty of stretch.

YARN
Pattons Classic Wool (100% pure new wool; 210 yd/192 m; 100 g/3.5 oz)

A: dark grey mix (2 skeins)
B: burgundy (1 skein)

NEEDLES
1 set size 3/3.25 mm straight needles *or size needed to obtain gauge*

NOTIONS
Cable needle
2 stitch holders or pieces of scrap yarn
Yarn needle

MEASUREMENTS
Small: 7" long
Medium: 8" long
Large: 10" long

GAUGE
5 sts / 8 rows = 1"

SPECIAL STITCH
Cable 8 back (C8B): Slip next 4 sts to cable needle and hold at back of work, k next 4 sts, k 4 sts from cable needle.

PATTERN

Instructions are for small size; instructions for medium and large are in brackets.

RIGHT MITTEN

Cuff

With B, cast on 40 {45, 50} sts. Knit 4 rows. Break off B; join A.

Row 1 (RS): With A, knit.

Row 2: *P2, k3; repeat from * to end.

Row 3: *P3, k2; repeat from * to end.

Repeat rows 2 and 3 until you have 15 {17, 19} total rows of ribbing; end with a WS row.

Dec row: *P1, p2tog, k2; repeat from * to end. (32 {36, 40} sts)

Work p2, k2 ribbing for 5 {7, 9} rows.

Hand

Row 1 (small size only): K2tog, k2, p2, kfb in each of next 2 sts, k4, p2, k17, kfb. (34 sts)

Row 1 (medium size only): K4, p2, kfb in each of next 2 sts, k4, p2, k22. (38 sts)

Row 1 (large size only): Kfb, k3, p2, kfb in each of next 2 sts, k4, p2, k24, k2tog. (42 sts)

Row 2 (all sizes): P19 {22, 25}, k2, p8, k2, p3 {4, 5}.

Row 3: K3 {4, 5}, p2; C8B; p2, knit to end.

Row 4: Repeat row 2.

Row 5: K3 {4, 5}, p2, k8, p2, k19 {22, 25}.

Row 6: Repeat row 2.

Row 7: K3 {4, 5}, p2, k8, p2, k2 {3, 4}, kfb in each of next 2 sts for thumb, k to end. (36 {40, 44} sts)

Row 8: P21 {24, 27}, k2, p8, k2, p3 {4, 5}.

Row 9: K3 {4, 5}, p2, k8, p2, k2 {3, 4}, kfb, k2, kfb, k to end. (38 {42, 46} sts)

Continue in this pattern, increasing 2 sts for the thumb in every odd row, having 2 more sts between the increases each time, for 6 {7, 8} total increase rows; work the cable twist (as in row 3) in every 10th row (i.e. row 13, row 23, etc.) to the end of the mitten.

Work 1 row even after last increase row. (46 {52, 58} sts)

Dividing row: Work 18 {20, 22} sts, slip onto stitch holder or piece of scrap yarn for back of hand, knit 13 {15, 17} sts for thumb, slip rem sts onto a second stitch holder or piece of yarn for palm.

Thumb

Work in stockinette st for 1¼ {1¾, 2¼} inches, ending with a knit row.

Dec row: P1, p2tog 6 {7, 8} times. (7 {8, 9} sts)

Break yarn, draw end twice through rem sts. Sew edges of thumb tog.

Hand Finishing

Take up sts for back of hand; join yarn, pick up and knit 2 sts at base of thumb, take up and k sts for palm of hand. (35 {39, 43} sts)

Work even until 3¾ {4¾, 5¾} inches above cuff, continuing to repeat cable twist every 10th row. End with a cable twist row.

Dec row 1: P3, *p2tog, p2; repeat from * to end. (27 {30, 33} sts)

Knit 1 row even.

Dec row 2: *P1, p2tog; repeat from * to end. (18 {20, 22} sts)

Knit 1 row even.

Dec row 2: P2tog across.

Break yarn, draw end twice through rem sts, and pull tight. Sew side seam and weave in all ends.

LEFT MITTEN

Cuff

With B, cast on 40 {45, 50} sts. Knit 4 rows garter st. Break off.

Row 1 (RS): With A, knit.

Row 2: *K3, p2; repeat from * to end.

Row 3: *K2, p3; repeat from * to end.

Repeat rows 2 and 3 until you have 15 {17, 19} total rows of ribbing; end with a WS row.

Dec row: *P1, p2tog, k2; repeat from * to end. (32 {36, 40} sts)

Work p2, k2 ribbing for 5 {7, 9} rows.

Hand

Row 1 (small size only): Inc 1 st in first st, k17, p2, inc 1 st in each of next 2 sts, k4, p2, k2, k2tog. (34 sts)

Row 1 (medium size only): K22, p2, inc 1 st in each of next 2 sts, k4, p2, k4. (38 sts)

Row 1 (large size only): K2tog, k24, p2, inc 1 st in each of next 2 sts, k4, p2, k3, inc 1 st in last st. (42 sts)

Row 2 (all sizes): P3 {4, 5}, k2, p8, k2, p19 {22, 25}.

Row 3: K19 {22, 25}, p2, C8B, work to end.

Continue to work as for right mitten up to dividing row.

Dividing row: K15 {17, 19}, slip these sts to a stitch holder or piece of scrap yarn for palm. Knit next 13 {15, 17} sts for thumb. Slip rem sts to a second holder or piece of yarn for back of hand.

Finish as for right mitten.

Pennsylvania Mittens

SKILL LEVEL

■■■■

EXPERIENCED

Fair Isle knitting gets a folk art twist in these patterned mittens. The intricate designs take some careful knitting, but the finished mittens are lovely and well worth the effort. As with other stranded colorwork, the double thickness of yarn means double warmth!

Fine

YARN
Knit Picks Stroll Sport (75% superwash merino wool, 25% nylon; 137 yd; 50 g) in
A: navy (2 skeins)
B: peapod (1 skein)

NEEDLES
1 set size 2/2.75 mm double-pointed needles
 or size needed to obtain gauge

NOTIONS
Scrap yarn

MEASUREMENTS
12" long

GAUGE
8 sts / 9 rows = 1"

PATTERN

RIGHT MITTEN

Cuff

With A, cast on 56 sts, divide on 3 needles, join.
Mark end of rounds throughout mitten. Work k
2, p 2 ribbing, working stripes as follows: 7
rounds A, 2 rounds B, 2 rounds A, 2 rounds B, 2
rounds A, 4 rounds B, 2 rounds A, 2 rounds B, 2
rounds A, 2 rounds B, 4 rounds A.

Hand

Inc Round: With A, *k 27, inc 1 st in next st; repeat
from * once. (58 sts)

> **Always carry yarn not in use loosely on wrong side
> of work, catching it up every 3rd st to avoid
> long loops on the inside of the mitten.**

Begin Fair Isle pattern:
Round 1: K 1 with A, k 1 with B for edge of thumb
gusset (see chart for thumb), k 3 A, k 1 B for 2nd
edge of thumb gusset. Follow chart for hand,
beginning with 7th st of round.
Round 2: Repeat round 1 (but use round 2 of the
charts).
Round 3: Repeat round 1 (but use round 3 of the
charts).
Round 4: K 1 A, k 1 B, k 1 A, make 1 A, k 1 A, make 1
A, k 1 A, k 1 B (7 sts in thumb gusset); work
remaining sts following round 4 of the hand
chart, beginning with 7th st of round.
Continue to follow both charts, increasing 1 st after
first A st and last A st of thumb gusset every 3rd
round 3 times more. (13 sts in thumb gusset)
Continue pattern with 13 sts in thumb gusset and
53 sts in remainder of hand until there are 23
pattern rounds in all.

Round 24: K 1 A, place next 13 thumb sts on a strand of yarn. With a separate strand of A, cast on 5 sts on left-hand needle; work these 5 sts following hand chart, beginning with 2nd st of chart. (58 sts in hand)

Round 25–55: K across, following the chart for the hand only.

Round 56: *Palm.* Following chart, k 1 A; k 1 B; with A, k2tog, inserting needle in back of sts. Work across chart until last 4 sts of palm; then with A, k2tog, inserting needle in front of sts, k 1 B, k 1 A. *Back of hand.* K 1 B; with A, k2tog, inserting needle in back of sts; work across chart until last 3 sts of back of hand; with A, k2tog, inserting needle in back of sts, k 1 B.

Round 57–63: Repeat round 56. (26 sts at end of round 63)

Round 64: *Palm.* K 1 A, K 1 B; with B, k2tog, inserting needle in back of sts. Work across chart until last 4 sts of palm; then with B, k2tog, inserting needle in front of sts, k 1 B, k 1 A. *Back of hand.* K 1 B; with B, k2tog, inserting needle in back of sts; work across chart until last 3 sts of back of hand; with B, k2tog, inserting needle in back of sts, k 1 B. (22 sts)

Round 65: *Palm.* With A, k 2; k2tog, inserting needle in back of sts; k 3; k2tog, inserting needle in front of sts; k 2. *Back of hand.* Still with A, k 1; k2tog, inserting needle in back of sts; k 5; k2tog, inserting needle in back of sts; k 1. (18 sts)

Split the 18 sts between two needles and weave together using kitchener stitch with A.

THUMB

Round 24: Slip the 13 thumb sts to 2 needles. With another needle and A, pick up and k 11 sts on the 5 cast-on sts; continue around, following chart, working 24th round on the 13 sts of the thumb. (11 sts on first needle, 7 sts on second needle, 6 sts on third needle: 24 sts)

Rounds 25–42: K around, following chart.

Round 43: Slip first st (border st) of second needle to first needle (12 sts on first needle, 6 sts on each of second and third needles). *With A, k2tog, inserting needle in back of sts; work to within 2 sts of next border st; k2tog; k 1 B. Repeat from * once. (20 sts)

Round 44: *With A, k2tog, inserting needle in back of sts; work to within 2 sts of next border st; k2tog; k 1 B. Repeat from * once. (16 sts)

Rounds 45–46: Repeat round 44.

Transfer sts from third needle to second needle (4 sts on each of two needles). With A, weave sts tog using kitchener stitch.

LEFT MITTEN

Work cuff and inc. round as for right mitten.

Begin Fair Isle pattern:

Round 1: Follow chart for first 23 sts, then k 1 B, k 3 A, k 1 B for thumb; finish round, following hand chart on page 100.

Continue to knit the mitten, replacing the stitches in the left box on the hand chart with the stitches from the thumb chart. After round 24, finish hand and thumb as for right mitten.

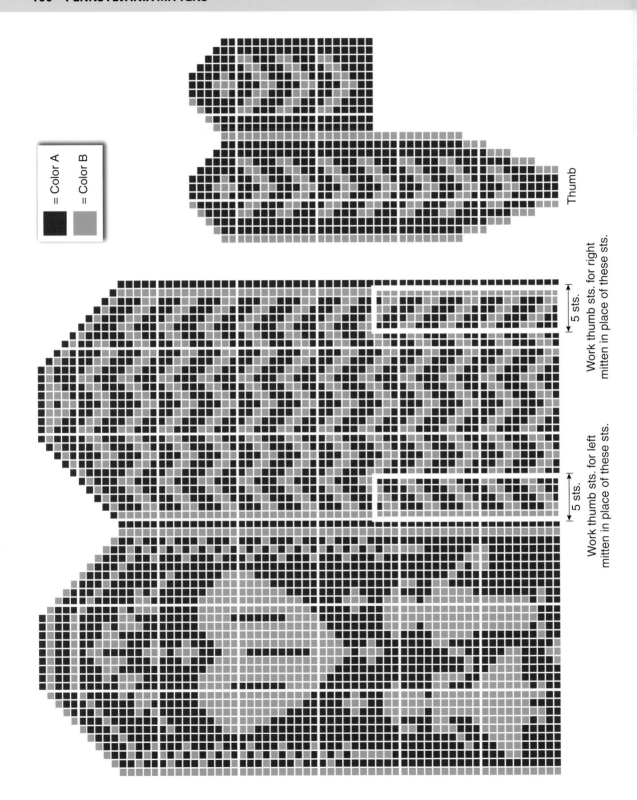

= Color A

= Color B

Thumb

5 sts.

Work thumb sts. for right mitten in place of these sts.

5 sts.

Work thumb sts. for left mitten in place of these sts.

Red Pepper Mittens

SKILL LEVEL

EASY

Sometimes you're just looking for a quick, easy mitten pattern with a little bit of simple decoration—and these bright, bulky mittens fit the bill! The thick yarn makes them extra fast to knit up, and the patterned panel on the backs of the hands adds a bit of interest without bringing up the difficulty of the project.

YARN
Lamb's Pride Bulky (85% wool,
15% mohair; 125 yd/114 m;
4 oz/113 g) in red hot passion
(1 skein)

NOTIONS
Stitch holders or pieces of scrap yarn (2)
Yarn needle

MEASUREMENTS
10¼" long

NEEDLES
1 set size 8/5 mm straight needles *or size
needed to obtain gauge*

GAUGE
3 sts / 5 rows = 1"

PATTERN

RIGHT MITTEN
Cuff
Cast on 24 sts.
Row 1 (RS): K4, (p1, k1) twice, p1, k15.
Row 2 (WS): P15, (p1, k1) twice, p1, p4.
Repeat rows 1 and 2 until the piece measures 3
   inches; end with a WS row.

Thumb Gusset
Row 1: K4, (p1, k1) twice, p1, k4, M1, k1, M1, k10.
Row 2: P17, (p1, k1) twice, p1, p4.
Row 3: K4, (p1, k1) twice, p1, k4, M1, k3, M1, k10.
Row 4: P19, (p1, k1) twice, p1, p4.
Row 5: K4, (p1, k1) twice, p1, k4, M1, k5, M1, k10.
Row 6: P21, (p1, k1) twice, p1, p4.
Row 7: K4, (p1, k1) twice, p1, k4, M1, k7, M1, k10.
Row 8: P23, (p1, k1) twice, p1, p4.
Row 9: K4, (p1, k1) twice, p1, k23.
Row 10: P23, (p1, k1) twice, p1, p4.
Dividing row: K4, (p1, k1) twice, p1, k4, place these
   sts on a stitch holder or piece of scrap yarn; k9;
   place rem sts on another stitch holder.

Thumb
Cast on 1 st at end of 9 thumb sts. Turn and purl
   back across these 10 sts; cast on 1 st at this end
   of thumb. (11 sts in thumb)
Work these 11 sts in stockinette st for 10 rows.
Dec row: K2tog across.
Break yarn, pull through rem sts, and fasten off. Sew
   up the thumb.

Hand
Place the sts from the first stitch holder back on the
   needle. Join yarn and pick up and knit 4 sts
   along base of thumb, then take up and work the
   sts from the second stitch holder.

Work these sts in the pattern until the mitten
   measures 3 3/4 inches from the picked-up sts
   along the bottom of the thumb.
Dec row 1: K1, ssk, k7, k2tog, k2, ssk, k8, k2tog.
Next row: Purl.
Dec row 2: K1, ssk, k5, k2tog, k2, ssk, k6, k2tog.
Next row: Purl
Dec row 3: K1, ssk, k3, k2tog, k2, ssk, k4, k2tog.
Next row: Purl.
Last row: K2tog across.
Break yarn, drawn through rem sts, and fasten off.
   Sew side seam and weave in ends.

LEFT MITTEN
Cuff
Cast on 24 sts.
Row 1 (RS): K15, (p1, k1) twice, p1, k4.
Row 2 (WS): P4, (p1, k1) twice, p1, p15.
Repeat rows 1 and 2 until the piece measures 3
   inches; end with a WS row.

Thumb Gusset
Row 1: K10, M1, k1, M1, k4, (p1, k1) twice, p1, k4.
Row 2: P4, (p1, k1) twice, p1, p17.
Row 3: K10, M1, k3, M1, k4, (p1, k1) twice, p1, k4.
Row 4: P4, (p1, k1) twice, p1, p19.
Row 5: K10, M1, k5, M1, k4, (p1, k1) twice, p1, k4.
Row 6: P4, (p1, k1) twice, p1, p21.
Row 7: K10, M1, k7, M1, k4, (p1, k1) twice, p1, k4.
Row 8: P4, (p1, k1) twice, p1, p23.
Row 9: K23, (p1, k1) twice, p1, k4.

Row 10: P4, (p1, k1) twice, p1, p23.
Dividing row: K10, place these sts on a stitch holder
    or piece of scrap yarn; k9; place rem sts on
    another stitch holder.
Finish as for right mitten.

Resources

SKILL LEVELS FOR KNITTING

1	◖□□□▷	**Beginner**	Projects for first-time knitters using basic knit and purl stitches. Minimal shaping.
2	◖■□□▷	**Easy**	Projects using basic stitches, repetitive stitch patterns, simple color changes, and simple shaping and finishing.
3	◖■■□▷	**Intermediate**	Projects with a variety of stitches, such as basic cables and lace, simple intarsia, double-pointed needles and knitting in the round needle techniques, mid-level shaping and finishing.
4	◖■■▶	**Experienced**	Projects using advanced techniques and stitches, such as short rows, Fair Isle, more intricate intarsia, cables, lace patterns, and numerous color changes.

This Standards & Guidelines booklet and downloadable symbol artwork are available at: **YarnStandards.com**

STANDARDS & GUIDELINES FOR CROCHET AND KNITTING

Standard Yarn Weight System

Categories of yarn, gauge ranges, and recommended needle and hook sizes

Yarn Weight Symbol & Category Names	0 Lace	1 Super Fine	2 Fine	3 Light	4 Medium	5 Bulky	6 Super Bulky
Type of Yarns in Category	Fingering 10 count crochet thread	Sock, Fingering, Baby	Sport, Baby	DK, Light Worsted	Worsted, Afghan, Aran	Chunky, Craft, Rug	Bulky, Roving
Knit Gauge Range* in Stockinette Stitch to 4 inches	33–40** sts	27–32 sts	23–26 sts	21–24 sts	16–20 sts	12–15 sts	6–11 sts
Recommended Needle in Metric Size Range	1.5–2.25 mm	2.25–3.25 mm	3.25–3.75 mm	3.75–4.5 mm	4.5–5.5 mm	5.5–8 mm	8 mm and larger
Recommended Needle U.S. Size Range	000 to 1	1 to 3	3 to 5	5 to 7	7 to 9	9 to 11	11 and larger
Crochet Gauge* Ranges in Single Crochet to 4 inch	32-42 double crochets**	21–32 sts	16–20 sts	12–17 sts	11–14 sts	8–11 sts	5–9 sts
Recommended Hook in Metric Size Range	Steel*** 1.6–1.4mm Regular hook 2.25 mm	2.25–3.5 mm	3.5–4.5 mm	4.5–5.5 mm	5.5–6.5 mm	6.5–9 mm	9 mm and larger
Recommended Hook U.S. Size Range	Steel*** 6, 7, 8 Regular hook B–1	B–1 to E–4	E–4 to 7	7 to I–9	I–9 to K–10½	K–10½ to M–13	M–13 and larger

* GUIDELINES ONLY: The above reflect the most commonly used gauges and needle or hook sizes for specific yarn categories.

** Lace weight yarns are usually knitted or crocheted on larger needles and hooks to create lacy, openwork patterns. Accordingly, a gauge range is difficult to determine. Always follow the gauge stated in your pattern.

*** Steel crochet hooks are sized differently from regular hooks--the higher the number, the smaller the hook, which is the reverse of regular hook sizing.

This Standards & Guidelines booklet and downloadable symbol artwork are available at: **YarnStandards.com**

Visual Index

Midwinter
Mittens
page 55

Midnight Mittens
page 79

Oslo Mittens
page 59

Annika Mittens
page 83

Checkerboard
Mittens
page 63

September
Gloves
page 87

Icicle Mittens
page 67

Snowball Fight
Mittens
page 91

Raspberry Sorbet
Gloves
page 71

Pennsylvania
Mittens
page 95

Peach Blossom
Baby Mittens
page 76

Red Pepper
Mittens
page 101